REVIEW OF THE ADB CLEAN ENERGY PROGRAM

MARCH 2020

ASIAN DEVELOPMENT BANK

 Creative Commons Attribution 3.0 IGO license (CC BY 3.0 IGO)

© 2020 Asian Development Bank
6 ADB Avenue, Mandaluyong City, 1550 Metro Manila, Philippines
Tel +63 2 8632 4444; Fax +63 2 8636 2444
www.adb.org

Some rights reserved. Published in 2020.

ISBN 978-92-9262-065-3 (print), 978-92-9262-066-0 (electronic); 978-92-9262-067-7 (ebook)
Publication Stock No. TCS200102-2
DOI: http://dx.doi.org/10.22617/TCS200102-2

The views expressed in this publication are those of the authors and do not necessarily reflect the views and policies of the Asian Development Bank (ADB) or its Board of Governors or the governments they represent.

ADB does not guarantee the accuracy of the data included in this publication and accepts no responsibility for any consequence of their use. The mention of specific companies or products of manufacturers does not imply that they are endorsed or recommended by ADB in preference to others of a similar nature that are not mentioned.

By making any designation of or reference to a particular territory or geographic area, or by using the term "country" in this document, ADB does not intend to make any judgments as to the legal or other status of any territory or area.

This work is available under the Creative Commons Attribution 3.0 IGO license (CC BY 3.0 IGO) https://creativecommons.org/licenses/by/3.0/igo/. By using the content of this publication, you agree to be bound by the terms of this license. For attribution, translations, adaptations, and permissions, please read the provisions and terms of use at https://www.adb.org/terms-use#openaccess.

This CC license does not apply to non-ADB copyright materials in this publication. If the material is attributed to another source, please contact the copyright owner or publisher of that source for permission to reproduce it. ADB cannot be held liable for any claims that arise as a result of your use of the material.

Please contact pubsmarketing@adb.org if you have questions or comments with respect to content, or if you wish to obtain copyright permission for your intended use that does not fall within these terms, or for permission to use the ADB logo.

Corrigenda to ADB publications may be found at http://www.adb.org/publications/corrigenda.

Notes:
In this publication, "$" refers to United States dollars.
ADB recognizes "China" as the People's Republic of China, "Korea" as the Republic of Korea, and "Bangalore" as Bengaluru

Cover design by Patrick Francisco.

Contents

Tables, Figures, and Boxes ... v

Foreword ... vi

Acknowledgments ... vii

Abbreviations ... viii

Executive Summary ... x

1 Introduction ... 1
   1.1 Guiding Principles for Energy Sector Operations: ADB Strategic Framework and Energy Policy ... 1
   1.2 Global Commitments ... 6

2 Conceptual Framework, Scope, and Limitations ... 7

3 Methodology and Data Sources ... 9

4 Elements and Approaches of the ADB Clean Energy Program ... 10
   4.1 Asia Solar Energy Initiative ... 10
   4.2 Carbon Capture and Storage ... 11
   4.3 Quantum Leap in Wind ... 11
   4.4 Small Wind Initiative ... 12
   4.5 Energy for All Initiative ... 12
   4.6 Asia Energy Efficiency Accelerator ... 13
   4.7 Low-Carbon Technology Exchange ... 13
   4.8 Asia Climate Change and Clean Energy Venture Capital Initiative ... 14
   4.9 Leveraging Clean Energy Development ... 14
   4.10 Knowledge Sharing and Partnerships ... 15

5 The ADB Clean Energy Program, 2008–2018 ... 17

6 Clean Energy Program Results, 2008–2018 ... 24

7 Findings and Conclusion ... 31

Appendixes

1	Clean Energy Projects (2008–2018)	33
2	ADB Projects with Energy Access Component (2008–2018)	55
3	Solar Projects Supported Under Asia Solar Energy Initiative (2010–2018)	66

References   **70**

Tables, Figures, and Boxes

Tables

1	Outline of Energy Sector Contribution to ADB's Operational Priorities	5
2	Results Framework of the 2009 ADB Energy Policy Implementation	8
3	Clean Energy and Climate Finance Monitoring Methodologies, Scope, and Application	17
4	Summary of Clean Energy Program Achievements by Energy Policy Results Framework Indicator	30

Figures

1	Review of the Clean Energy Program–Conceptual Framework	7
2	Clean Energy Investments by Category, 2008–2018	18
3	Clean Energy Investments by Operations, 2008–2018	19
4	Clean Energy Investments by Renewable Energy Technology, 2008–2018	20
5	Energy Efficiency Investments by Type, 2008–2018	20
6	ADB Energy Access Investment and Improved Energy Access, 2003–2018	21
7	Energy Access by Operations, 2008–2018	22
8	ADB Energy Access Investment by Category, 2008–2018	22
9	Energy Access Investments in Clean Cooking, Heating, and Improvement of District Heating Systems, 2008–2018	23
10	Clean Energy Investments, 2008–2018	25
11	Additional Capacity Using Renewable Energy, 2008–2018	26
12	Electricity Savings, 2008–2018	27
13	CO_2 Emission Reduction, 2008–2018	28
14	Energy Access Projects, 2008–2018	28
15	Energy Access Investments, 2008–2018	29
16	New and Improved Electricity Connection, 2008–2018	29

Foreword

The review of the Clean Energy Program of the Asian Development Bank (ADB) looks back into a decade's worth of ADB projects that supported renewable energy generation, energy efficiency, and cleaner fuel. It examines ADB's achievements against the targets set under the results framework of its 2009 Energy Policy. The targets include minimum annual investments in clean energy projects, capacity installed using renewable energy, electricity saved, carbon dioxide emissions reduced, and number of households provided with new and improved electricity connections. It also explores what ADB needs to do to stay relevant amid the evolving operational context to support the ADB Strategy 2030, and the global commitments of the Sustainable Development Goals and the Paris Agreement.

The ADB Clean Energy Program seeks to increase efficiency in energy, transport, and urban development; help countries adopt renewable energy sources; and improve access to energy particularly for poor and remote regions. Between 2008 and 2018, ADB invested $2 billion annually on average, which met the minimum annual target set for 2013 onward. A total of $22.12 billion was invested in clean energy for 2008–2018, of which 58.7% was in renewable energy, 38.0% in energy efficiency, and 3.3% in cleaner fuel. For the same period, over 22 million households were provided with new and improved electricity connections, and a cumulative reduction of 144.25 million tons of carbon dioxide equivalent was registered from the clean energy projects.

The targets under the 2009 Energy Policy Results Framework were mostly achieved. While ADB invested considerably in renewable energy and energy access projects, investments for energy efficiency need to be further expanded which will in turn, sustain the outcomes of renewable energy and energy access projects. Aside from the electricity sector, more efforts in efficient and cleaner heating, cooling, and cooking will help better living conditions and increase the region's mileage in providing modern energy access and reducing carbon emissions.

This review of the Clean Energy Program is a good reference on the performance of ADB energy projects and shows that the ADB energy sector can effectively contribute to providing affordable, reliable, sustainable, and modern energy for all; combating climate change; pursuing a sustainable low-carbon future; and achieving a prosperous, inclusive, resilient, and sustainable Asia and the Pacific.

Woochong Um
Director General
Sustainable Development and Climate Change Department
Asian Development Bank

Acknowledgments

The *Review of the ADB Clean Energy Program* is an output of a comprehensive study carried out by the Sustainable Development and Climate Change Department (SDCC) of the Asian Development Bank (ADB). The study was conducted by a team in the Sector Advisory Service Cluster–Energy Sector Group (SDSC-ENE) led by Kee-Yung Nam, principal energy economist under the overall guidance of Yongping Zhai, chief of Energy Sector Group and Robert Guild, chief sector officer.

The main contributing authors of the review are Charity L. Torregosa, senior energy officer, SDCC, with consultants Fely Arriola, Lyndree Malang, and Pil Bae Song. Charity L. Torregosa coordinated the production and worked with Ma. Theresa Mercado (copy editor and proofreader), Patrick Francisco (cover designer), Edith Creus (layout artist), Anthony H. Victoria, Cynthia A. Hidalgo, Noren M. Jose, and Rodel S. Bautista of the Department of Communications. Staff support was also provided by Cimonette Caguioa, Gervic Laurio, Daisy Salgado, Marcial Semira, and Ana Maria Tolentino (consultants).

Appreciation and gratitude are extended to other colleagues who provided comments, inputs, and insights from operations, namely Andrew Jeffries and Olly Norojono.

Abbreviations

ACEF	Asia Clean Energy Forum
ADB	Asian Development Bank
ADF	Asian Development Fund
ASEI	Asia Solar Energy Initiative
ASEF	Asia Solar Energy Forum
CCS	carbon capture and storage
CCSF	Carbon Capture and Storage Fund
CEF	Clean Energy Fund
CEFPF	Clean Energy Financing Partnership Facility
CER	certified emission reduction
CFPS	Canadian Climate Fund for the Private Sector in Asia
CO_2	carbon dioxide
COP	Conference of the Parties
CWRD	Central and West Asia Department
DMC	developing member country
DSEE	demand-side energy efficiency
EARD	East Asia Department
EE	energy efficiency
ESCO	Energy Service Company
FCF	Future Carbon Fund
GGGI	Global Green Growth Institute
GHG	greenhouse gas
IEA	International Energy Agency
IED	Independent Evaluation Department
IRENA	International Renewable Energy Agency
KEA	Korea Energy Agency
LAO PDR	Lao People's Democratic Republic
LCT	low-carbon technology
LED	light-emitting diode
LPG	liquefied petroleum gas
MDG	Millennium Development Goal
NDC	nationally determined contribution
NEDO	New Energy and Industrial Technology Development Organization
NPS	new policies scenario
OBA	output-based assistance

OPIC	Overseas Private Investment Corporation
PARD	Pacific Department
PaYG	pay-as-you-go
PNG	Papua New Guinea
PPP	purchasing power parity
PRC	People's Republic of China
PSOD	Private Sector Operations Department
RRP	report and recommendation of the President
SARD	South Asia Department
SDG	Sustainable Development Goal
SDS	sustainable development scenario
SEAS	Sustainable Energy Association of Singapore
SEforAll	Sustainable Energy for All
SERD	Southeast Asia Department
TA	technical assistance
UNESCAP	United Nations Economic and Social Commission for Asia and the Pacific
UNDP	United Nations Development Programme
UNFCCC	United Nations Framework Convention on Climate Change
USAID	United States Agency for International Development
WEC	World Energy Council

Weights and Measures

$GTCO_2$	gigatons CO_2
GW	gigawatt
GWh	gigawatt-hour
kW	kilowatt
kWh	kilowatt-hour
MJ	megajoule
$MtCO_2$	million tons carbon dioxide
MW	megawatt
tCO_{2-eq}	tons of carbon dioxide equivalent
TJ	terajoule
TWh	terawatt-hour

Executive Summary

The energy sector in the Asia and Pacific region continues to face daunting challenges. The region needs stable, reliable, and affordable energy supply to continue its rapid economic growth and provide modern forms of energy to millions of its population in a sustainable manner. The operations of the Asian Development Bank (ADB) have, since 2009, been guided by an Energy Policy based on three operational pillars of (i) promoting energy efficiency and renewable energy; (ii) maximizing access to energy for all; and (iii) promoting energy sector reform, capacity building, and governance. The Clean Energy Program embodies—and is among the vehicles to achieve—the goals of the Energy Policy 2009. From previous initiatives before its formal articulation in 2011, the Clean Energy Program was designed to consist of both direct and leverage financing, capacity building, knowledge sharing, and technology exchange. This review assesses the ADB Clean Energy Program against output indicators in the 2009 Energy Policy.

The Clean Energy Program achieved the clean energy investment target of $2 billion during 2008–2018 on average, and in every year during 2008–2017. The clean energy investment in 2018 declined to $1.4 billion, reflecting a global trend of cost reduction of renewable energy such as solar photovoltaic (PV) and onshore wind in particular. Moreover, as renewable energy is increasingly competitive vis-à-vis conventional power generation, private investors and commercial banks have become the main sources of funding, while ADB has increased its financing in electricity transmission and distribution systems that can integrate more renewable energy. The targets for each indicator of the Clean Energy Program were met, exceeding the 2005–2007 baseline except for the annual electricity savings due to the challenges of implementing demand-side energy efficiency projects.

For 2008–2018, cumulative investments in clean energy amounted to $22.12 billion. Investments in renewable energy had the biggest share at 58.7% of the total, while energy efficiency had 38.0%, and cleaner fuel 3.3%. Cumulative investments in energy access amounted to $9.02 billion, and over 22 million households were given new or improved electricity connections. For all the clean energy projects, cumulative carbon emission reduction was 144.25 million tons of carbon dioxide equivalent (tCO2-eq). A total of 384 clean energy projects were reviewed for this report. The achievements by indicator are summarized below:

(i) Clean energy investments averaged $2.01 billion annually during the review period;
(ii) The average renewable energy capacity added per year is 1.29 gigawatts (GW) exceeding the baseline of 0.47 GW;
(iii) Average annual electricity savings was 3.73 terrawatt-hours (TWh) per year, falling short of the baseline of 9.8 TWh per year;
(iv) CO_2 emissions averaged 13.11 million tons of CO_2 equivalent (tCO_2-eq) annually, surpassing the baseline of 8.20 million tCO_2-eq every year;
(v) Energy access projects increased from the baseline of 4 to an average of 13 per year;

(vi) Energy access investments averaged $820 million per year, surpassing the baseline of $140.45 million; and

(vii) The annual average number of households given new and improved electricity connections is 2 billion, exceeding the baseline of 253,847 households.

As guided by the 2009 Energy Policy, ADB's energy sector operations and its Clean Energy Program remain relevant to and address the demands and requirements of Strategy 2030, energy-related Sustainable Development Goals, and the Paris Agreement. Scaling up of support for climate change, disaster resilience, and environmental sustainability are among the key priority activities of the ADB Strategy 2030. ADB is committed to ensure that 75% of the number of its committed operations on a 3-year rolling average will be supporting climate change mitigation and adaptation by 2030, targeting to invest $80 billion in climate finance from 2019 to 2030.

1 Introduction

The Asia and Pacific region has, in recent years, become the fastest growing region in the world, bringing with it increased energy consumption and the attendant greenhouse gas (GHG) emissions. The region sits at a critical juncture in the fight against climate change, where it could make substantial dents in the global GHG emissions, effectively change the dynamic between economic growth and energy use, and steer regional development toward a sustainable low-carbon path.

The Asian Development Bank (ADB) has framed its support for its developing member countries (DMCs) according to its DMCs' needs. The focus, objective, and approaches the organization has employed throughout its 50 years have also evolved according to the call and demands of the times. From the very first energy sector loan in 1969 for diesel-powered generation in Malaysia for $3.1 million, ADB's portfolio in the sector has grown immensely to billions and has been reoriented toward cleaner and more sustainable investments amid the threat of worsening impacts of climate change. Energy sector operations hover from 23% to 25% of total ADB lending throughout ADB's history, except during 1997–2006 when it only accounted for 15%. The energy sector remains to date, one of the major sectors in ADB operations in terms of lending volume, along with the transport sector. It is thus significant in determining the characteristic and direction of ADB lending. While a large part of ADB's energy portfolio is still allocated to transmission and distribution projects, it has been mainstreaming renewable energy generation and energy efficiency in its investments through its Clean Energy Program since 2008. The program was developed to help ADB DMCs meet their energy security needs, provide reliable and affordable energy access, and help them transition to a low-carbon growth path.

Ten years hence, a look-back is in order: (i) to see how far the program has gone in terms of what it set out to do; (ii) draw lessons to guide current and future implementation; and (iii) identify further courses of action including new directions, targets, and approaches to enhance ADB's own institutional goals, effectively contribute to global commitments, and remain responsive to the needs of its DMCs in light of the evolving organizational and global contexts.

1.1 Guiding Principles for Energy Sector Operations: ADB Strategic Framework and Energy Policy

The energy sector operations in ADB has been guided throughout the years by an energy policy. The first energy policy was issued in 1981 to help DMCs respond to the global oil shocks of the 1970s, and set the framework for the overall energy sector operations to (i) develop energy infrastructure and indigenous energy sources, (ii) promote efficiency, and (iii) create markets conducive to foreign investment in DMCs.[1]

---

[1] ADB. 2009. *Energy Policy 2009*. June. Manila. https://www.adb.org/sites/default/files/institutional-document/32032/energy-policy-2009.pdf.

Since then, ADB's goals and objectives in its energy sector operations had taken its cue from the organization's overall strategic framework. The 1995 energy sector policy paper, whose three main thrusts were private sector development, improving energy efficiency, and integrating environmental considerations in energy development, was consistent with the Medium-Term Strategic Framework 1995–1998 that pursued economic growth, poverty reduction, human development, improvement of the status of women, and environmental protection.[2]

The 1995 Energy Policy also set the operating principles for energy sector projects: full cost recovery, reduction of subsidies, establishment of independent regulatory mechanisms, tariff-setting based on transparent principles, corporatization and privatization of government-owned utilities, and promotion of regional trade in energy, demand-side management, rural electrification, and renewable energy development. It was in the late 1990s that the overall focus of the energy sector was the restructuring of the power sector, expansion of power supply, and enhancement of the operational efficiency of power utilities.[3]

The first renewable energy project was approved in 1996. The $100 million loan helped the Government of India expand the development of four major renewable energy sources: bio-methanation for the production of energy, bagasse-based cogeneration of power, wind energy and solar-thermal system development; and help mainstream these renewable energy technologies. The loan that was on-lent to private entities at commercial terms was going to help generate about 126 megawatt (MW)-equivalent of new capacity from renewable energy, which will reduce the country's coal consumption by about 625,000 tons per year and improve air and water quality correspondingly.[4]

Five years into its implementation, the 1995 Energy Policy was reviewed in 2000 with the reaffirmation of the framework and objectives. It also recommended the development of independently regulated and privatized energy markets that could lead to more efficient uses of energy, lower costs, and encourage more private investments.[5]

Strategic Framework 2001. ADB formulated in 2001 its Long-Term Strategic Framework 2001–2015 to (i) promote environmentally sound development without compromise; and (ii) support overall economic efficiency to deliver sustainable economic growth and social development through good governance, increased sector-wide approaches to assistance, efficient use of capital, and competitive capital markets. The framework emphasized that ADB must ensure—in conjunction with its DMCs—that environmental policies adopt an integrated resource management approach, apart from advocating the integration of environmental policies and objectives into national development policies and objectives.[6] Recognizing the environmental considerations in development had further galvanized ADB's support for clean energy in the region. A program was launched to facilitate the development of renewable energy, energy efficiency, GHG abatement, and climate change adaptation in 2001 known as the Renewable Energy, Energy Efficiency, and Climate Change Program (REACH). It sought to build pipelines for renewable energy, energy efficiency, and climate change adaptation and mitigation projects in ADB. In 2002, the Government of the Netherlands contributed resources for the Promotion of Renewable Energy and Energy Efficiency and Greenhouse Gas Abatement (PREGA). These funding platforms supporting clean energy development would be the major catalysts for the program on clean energy that was slowly coming into form. In 2005, the Energy Efficiency Initiative was launched, which strengthened the

---

[2] ADB. *Asian Development Bank Annual Report 1995*. Manila. https://www.adb.org/sites/default/files/institutional-document/32137/adb-ar-1995.pdf.
[3] ADB. 1995. *Bank Policy for the Energy Sector*. Manila.
[4] ADB. *Asian Development Bank Annual Report 1996*. Manila. https://www.adb.org/sites/default/files/institutional-document/32136/adb-ar-1996.pdf.
[5] ADB. 2000. *Energy 2000 Review of the Energy Policy of the Asian Development Bank*. Manila.
[6] ADB. 2001. *Moving the Poverty Reduction Agenda Forward in Asia and the Pacific: The Long-Term Strategic Framework of the Asian Development Bank (2001–2015)*. Manila. http://hdl.handle.net/11540/5467.

institutional foundations to support clean energy investments. It was in 2005 that the annual target for clean energy investment was first set at $1 billion from 2008.[7]

In 2006, the first Asia Clean Energy Forum (ACEF) was held to provide a knowledge platform on clean energy in Asia and the Pacific. ACEF has since become one of ADB's flagship knowledge events that has continued to gather multisectoral stakeholders in the field of clean energy to exchange learning and latest information on technology, financing, and policy.

In 2007, ADB established the Clean Energy Financing Partnership Facility (CEFPF) that rationalized cofinancing bilateral resources in one financing platform to support clean energy development. CEFPF resources were further augmented with the inclusion of Japan's Asia Clean Energy Fund in 2008. The Energy for All Initiative was also launched in 2008, seeking to "develop new approaches, methodologies for promoting greater access to reliable, affordable modern energy for the region's poor." These initiatives became the precursors of what will be articulated in 2011 as the ADB Clean Energy Program, and also signified ADB's commitment to low-carbon growth.

Strategy 2020 or the Long-Term Strategic Framework (2008–2020) approved in April 2008 set the goals of ADB to fulfill its vision of an Asia and Pacific region free of poverty by 2020 according to the three complementary strategic agendas of (i) inclusive growth, (ii) environmentally and sustainable growth, and (iii) regional integration. To support the agenda under Strategy 2020, and effectively mobilize its resources and maximize the returns on its regional focus and expertise, ADB was to employ five drivers of change: (i) private sector development and private sector operations, (ii) good governance and capacity development, (iii) gender equity, (iv) knowledge solutions, and (v) partnerships, and refocus its efforts on five core specializations: infrastructure; environment, including climate change; regional cooperation and integration; financial sector development; and education.[8]

With Strategy 2020 in place, ADB set out to review the 1995 Energy Policy. One of the findings was that demand for primary energy in developing Asia would grow twice as much by 2030 with the People's Republic of China (PRC) and India accounting for the major share driven by rapid economic and population growth, urbanization, and replacement of noncommercial biomass fuels by commercial fuel. The estimated increase in energy demand was projected to be met largely by fossil fuels, presenting therefore, energy security and climate change risks.[9]

2009 Energy Policy. The review paved the way for the formulation of the 2009 Energy Policy that was approved in June of that year to respond to the changing dynamics in the sector and also align ADB energy sector operations with Strategy 2020. The 2009 Energy Policy mandated ADB to help its DMCs "to provide reliable, adequate, and affordable energy for inclusive growth" in a socially, economically, and environmentally sustainable manner. The implementation of the policy is guided by the following three pillars: (i) promoting energy efficiency and renewable energy; (ii) maximizing energy access for all; and (iii) promoting energy sector reform, capacity building, and governance. It set the target of investing $2 billion in clean energy projects annually starting 2013, which doubled from the $1 billion targeted annually from 2008.

Clean Energy Program. Through a memo dated 26 July 2011, the co-chairs of what then was known as the Energy Community of Practice, a full articulation of the ADB Clean Energy Program was circulated among ADB's

---

[7] ADB. 2015. *Clean Energy Program: Accelerating Low-Carbon Development in Asia and the Pacific Region - Brochure*. https://www.adb.org/sites/default/files/publication/28995/clean-energy-program-brochure.pdf.
[8] ADB. *2008 Strategy 2020: The Long-Term Strategic Framework of the Asian Development Bank 2008–2020*. Manila. https://www.adb.org/sites/default/files/institutional-document/32121/strategy2020-print.pdf.
[9] ADB. 2009. *Energy Policy*. Manila.

then operations departments and other Communities of Practice. The Clean Energy Program "aims to lower energy-related emissions (including carbon dioxide), extend supply of modern energy services to all, and improve economy-wide energy efficiency to effectively reduce the rate of growth of energy demand." Together, these objectives were to contribute to attaining energy security for ADB DMCs.

This articulation of the Clean Energy Program consolidated past initiatives in renewable energy, energy efficiency, and energy access in one cohesive program that outlines its thrusts, activities, scope, and approach, including identifying the various instruments to meet its objectives, and the risks that could affect its successful implementation. Also, in this articulation, clean energy investments were increased from $1 billion previously announced in 2005 to $2 billion in 2013, which is the target set in the 2009 Energy Policy.

The 2009 Energy Policy remained relevant after the midterm review (MTR) of Strategy 2020 in 2014. The MTR sharpened ADB's operational focus to better address the development challenges of transforming the region through (i) increased emphasis on inclusiveness, (ii) promoting innovation and resilience, and (iii) strengthening support for middle-income countries. The review also reiterated that the three strategic agendas of inclusive growth, environmental sustainability, and regional integration are crucial for the remaining period of Strategy 2020. It highlighted the importance of ADB's continued expansion of climate change and adaptation work, which entails continued support for clean energy and energy access. One crucial aspect that was emphasized in the MTR was innovation, which the energy sector and its operations have incorporated in the design, processes in project development and implementation, and its methods of work.

In September 2015, ADB climate finance targets were set with ADB aiming to invest $6 billion by 2020: $4 billion in mitigation and $2 billion in adaptation activities. The energy sector was to contribute $3 billion of climate mitigation investments while transport's share was $1 billion. Climate mitigation activities included expanding support for renewable energy, energy efficiency, sustainable transport, and building smart cities.

Strategy 2030. The ADB Board of Directors approved in July 2018 Strategy 2030 that sets the direction that ADB will take in the next decade. ADB will sustain its efforts to eradicate extreme poverty and expand its vision to achieve a prosperous, inclusive, resilient, and sustainable Asia and the Pacific, aligning its vision with major global commitments, including the United Nations' Sustainable Development Goals (SDGs), and the Paris Agreement on Climate Change. ADB will play a key role in supporting the global agenda of infrastructure development as a source of global growth. ADB will promote quality infrastructure investments that are green sustainable, resilient, and inclusive. Under Strategy 2030, ADB aims to have 75% of its committed investments allocated to climate finance, investing $80 billion cumulatively from 2019 to 2030.[10]

Among the principles embodied in the new strategy that have implications on its operations including the energy sector are: adding value to its DMCs by combining finance, knowledge, and partnerships; strengthening its country-focused approach using the country partnership strategy as the main platform to define customized support; and promoting the use of innovative technologies and delivering integrated solutions by combining expertise across a range of sectors and themes through a mix of public and private sector operations. ADB will prioritize support for the poorest and most vulnerable countries in the region, including fragile and conflict-affected situations and small island developing states.

---

[10] ADB. 2018. *Strategy 2030: Achieving a Prosperous, Inclusive, Resilient, and Sustainable Asia and the Pacific.* Manila. https://www.adb.org/sites/default/files/institutional-document/435391/strategy-2030-main-document.pdf.

ADB has identified the following operational priorities under Strategy 2030. These are

(i) Addressing remaining poverty and reducing inequalities;
(ii) Accelerating progress in gender equality;
(iii) Tackling climate change, building disaster resilience;
(iv) Making cities more livable;
(v) Promoting rural development and food security;
(vi) Strengthening governance and institutional capacity; and
(vii) Fostering regional cooperation and integration.

ADB developed operational plans for the seven priority areas that articulate the strategic focus, specific areas of engagement, approaches, and broad skills requirements to guide the implementation of the priority areas. A new corporate results framework has been developed and will be updated to monitor and measure implementation progress. ADB instituted a "One ADB" approach, bringing together knowledge and expertise across the organization to effectively implement Strategy 2030.

While not singled-out or emphasized, the energy sector, as one of the major sectors in ADB operations, will follow the refinements and articulation being undertaken by the Strategy 2030 processes. The energy sector has formulated its own operational approaches on how it will contribute, advance, and implement initiatives and activities to pursue the visions and goals set by Strategy 2030, as part of the process of the review of the 2009 Energy Policy conducted from 2019 to 2020. The 2009 Energy Policy has the basic elements to contribute to Strategy 2030 as shown in Table 1. This report will assess the achievements of the Clean Energy Program based on the Results Framework in the 2009 Energy Policy, identify general areas of intervention, enhancement, or development with regard to the objectives set in Strategy 2030, and the major global commitments such as the SDGs and the Paris Agreement.

Table 1: Outline of Energy Sector Contribution to ADB's Operational Priorities

Operational Priorities	Energy Sector Contributions
Addressing remaining poverty and reducing inequalities	Clean energy for meeting basic needs (lighting and cooking), skills development and job creation with renewable energy, productive use of energy to generate income
Accelerating progress in gender equality	Clean energy access relieves women of fuel collection, which allows women more time to pursue income-generating activities
Tackling climate change, building disaster resilience	Integrating climate change mitigation (greenhouse gas reduction) and adaptation into project design
Making cities more livable	Supporting smart electricity supply to cities, energy efficient buildings, and electric vehicles, rooftop solar for residential and commercial structures
Promoting rural development and food security	Supporting solar-powered pumps for smart irrigation to replace diesel or electricity-powered pumps
Strengthening governance and institutional capacity	Promoting energy sector reforms and developing institutional capacity for renewable energy development
Fostering regional cooperation and integration	Promoting energy connectivity (power interconnections, gas pipelines), and sharing best practices and technologies in renewable energy development

ADB = Asian Development Bank.
Source: ADB.

1.2 Global Commitments

Similar to many international development institutions, ADB operates in support of global initiatives such as the United Nations' SDGs and the Paris Agreement on Climate Change, among others. These agreements provide a set of common standards and achievable targets to end poverty, reduce carbon emissions, manage the risks of climate change and natural disasters, and build back better after a crisis.

1.2.1 Sustainable Development Goals

Building on the Millennium Development Goals (MDGs), the UN launched the 2030 Agenda for Sustainable Development and set 17 SDGs that encompass poverty alleviation and human development, climate change, economic inequality, innovation, sustainable consumption, peace, and justice. The SDGs are a universal call to action to end poverty, protect the planet, and ensure that all people enjoy peace and prosperity. ADB energy sector operations guided by its 2009 Energy Policy and further supported by the Clean Energy Program is aligned with and supports SDG 7. The specific targets under SDG 7 to be achieved by 2030 are (i) universal access to affordable, reliable, and modern energy services; (ii) increase substantially the share of renewable energy in the global energy mix; (iii) double the global rate of improvement in energy efficiency; (iv) enhance international cooperation to facilitate access to clean energy research and technology, including renewable energy, energy efficiency, and advanced cleaner fossil fuel technology, and promote investment in energy infrastructure and clean energy technology; and (v) expand infrastructure and upgrade technology for supplying modern and sustainable energy services for all in developing countries, in particular least developed countries, small island developing states and landlocked developing countries, in accordance with their respective programs of support.[11]

1.2.2 Paris Agreement

At the 21st Conference of the Parties in Paris, on 12 December 2015, Parties to the United Nations Framework Convention on Climate Change (UNFCCC) reached a landmark agreement to combat climate change and to accelerate and intensify the actions and investments needed for a sustainable low-carbon future. The aim of the Paris Agreement is to provide a stronger global response to combat the threat of climate change specifically by keeping global temperature rise this century below 2°C above pre-industrial levels and at the same time by pursuing efforts to limit further temperature increase to 1.5°C. It also intends to increase countries' abilities to deal with the impacts of climate change and by making climate finance flows consistent with low GHG emissions and climate-resilient pathways. To achieve such ambitious goals, the following are required and envisioned to be put in place to support developing countries and the most vulnerable countries, in line with their own national objectives:

(i) appropriate mobilization and provision of financial resources,
(ii) new technology and enhanced capacity building, and
(iii) enhanced transparency framework for action and support.

The agreement likewise entails all parties to show their strong commitment and efforts in the coming years through their respective "nationally determined contributions (NDCs)." Since April 2016, 185 Parties have ratified the Paris Agreement. The Paris Agreement's implications for the ADB energy sector is provision of support to its DMCs in all aspects: project financing, technology and knowledge transfer, and capacity building in meeting their NDCs.[12]

---

[11] United Nations. *Sustainable Development Goals*. https://www.un.org/sustainabledevelopment/sustainable-development-goals/.
[12] United Nations Framework Convention on Climate Change. The Paris Agreement. https://unfccc.int/process-and-meetings/the-paris-agreement/the-paris-agreement.

2 Conceptual Framework, Scope, and Limitations

ADB, its interventions, and support to its DMCs do not exist in a vacuum. The energy policies and specific projects and programs it has implemented were formulated based on its analysis of concrete conditions of the DMCs, extensive dialogue with its DMCs on their needs, existing plans, and future programs; and the overall global setting, which is dynamic and constantly changing. ADB has at its disposal various instruments and systems to keep abreast of these changes. This review is part of that process and will assess the Clean Energy Program based on the conceptual framework illustrated in Figure 1:

Figure 1: Review of the Clean Energy Program–Conceptual Framework

	2009 Energy Policy Results Framework	Strategy 2030	NDCs and SDGs
Achievements	■		
Gaps	■	■	■
New areas and directions		■	■

NDC = nationally determined contribution, SDG = Sustainable Development Goal.
Source: ADB.

The achievements of the program and the status of implementation of the Clean Energy Program will be measured against the relevant indicators set in the Results Framework of the 2009 Energy Policy. Gaps will be identified across the criteria and objectives set by the three aspects and levels of analysis: 2009 Energy Policy, Strategy 2030, and the global commitments (Paris Agreement and the SDGs). Lastly, new areas and directions will then be informed by the goals and objectives of the Strategy 2030 and the global commitments.

From the Results Framework of the 2009 Energy Policy, relevant in the review of the Clean Energy Program are outputs 1 and 2 using as the basis of measurement the corresponding indicator for each output. Table 2 shows the results framework and the scope of the review highlighted.

Table 2. Results Framework of the 2009 ADB Energy Policy Implementation

Output	Output Indicators
ADB investments in energy efficiency and renewable energy expanded	More than $2 billion annually will be invested from 2013, in US dollars
	Additional installed capacity using renewable energy, in megawatts (increase from baseline)
	Electricity saved per year, in gigawatt-hours (increase from baseline)
	Reduction of carbon dioxide emissions, ton of carbon dioxide equivalent avoided per year (increase from baseline)
ADB investments in electrification expanded	Number (increase from baseline)
	Amount, in US dollars (increase from baseline)
	Total additional installed capacity, in megawatts (increase from baseline)
	Number of new households connected to electricity (increase from baseline)
ADB support for reforms and capacity development expanded and effective	Level of approved investments • Number of loans and grants (increase from baseline) • Number of TA projects (increase from baseline) • Amount of loans and grants, in US dollars (increase from baseline) • Amount of TA projects, in US dollars (increase from baseline)
	Effectiveness of investments • Percentage of project completion reports rated satisfactory (maintain or improve depending on baseline) • Percentage of TA completion reports rated satisfactory (maintain or improve depending on baseline)

ADB = Asian Development Bank, TA = technical assistance, US = United States.
Source: ADB.

The review will cover 2008–2018, drawing secondary data from the clean energy and access projects approved during the period. A commentary on the overall design of the Clean Energy Program as articulated in 2011 will necessarily be part of the scope of the review with respect to how other initiatives, approaches, and other activities were implemented to support the program. The review will not include the organizational or institutional aspects of program implementation or its governance mechanisms.

ADB defines clean energy projects as loan investments and activities that result in reduced GHG emissions.[13] Greenfield power generation projects that use fossil fuels (including gas) are not considered clean energy projects as these are net positive emitters and will lock in emission impacts throughout the life of a plant. Retrofitting fossil fuel-based, however, fall within the scope of clean energy projects. Projects in energy efficiency, renewable energy generation, and switching to cleaner fuels whose outcome lead to the reduction of GHG emissions fall within the purview of this review. Energy access, on the other hand, addresses the energy, environment, and poverty nexus concerns by linking households to modern energy sources, technologies, and finance. Specifically, access to energy involves any or a combination of the following: (i) provision of electricity and motive power to households, (ii) improvement in the supply and delivery of energy services to households, (iii) provision of modern fuels and/or efficient devices for cooking and/or heating to households, and (iv) provision of finance to households to access energy. ADB uses this definition in the estimation of its investments in energy access.

---

[13] ADB. 2011. *Indicators for the Asian Development Bank Energy Sector Operations (2005–2010)*. https://www.adb.org/sites/default/files/publication/29435/indicators-energy-operations.pdf.

3 Methodology and Data Sources

Comparative and gap analyses will be employed to review the Clean Energy Program based on secondary information on investments in clean energy and energy access from 2008 to 2018, disaggregated by category, operations, technology, and the outcomes the projects seek to achieve.

The first level of analysis will compare the outcomes achieved by ADB investments in clean energy and energy access to indicators set in the 2009 Energy Policy Results Framework, that aims for an increase in all output indicators from the baseline. The baseline is the level of these indicators averaged from 2005 to 2007 energy sector operations data to be consistent with the methodology applied earlier in 2011.

The second level of analysis will generate any disparity between outcomes achieved over the 10-year period and to the goals and objectives of SDG 7, the Paris Agreement, and Strategy 2030 through a gap analysis, which will also help thresh out the future directions, approaches, and new initiatives that could be part of the Clean Energy Program.

The main sources of secondary data are ADB reports and data systems that include annual clean energy investments project summaries, reports and recommendations of the President, technical assistance (TA) reports, ADB publications, and internal reports issued by ADB on clean energy and energy access.

For clean energy, there were a total of 384 projects from 2008 to 2018 analyzed in this report; 295 come from the energy sector while 89 come from other sectors such as agriculture and natural resources, transport, urban, and water. Projects from other sectors that have clean energy components were included in the monitoring and reporting of clean energy investments from 2008 to 2015.

A total of 138 energy access projects were reviewed in this report from 2008 to 2018 including 125 projects from the energy sector and 13 from other sectors, comprising 36 TA projects and 102 investment projects.

4 Elements and Approaches of the ADB Clean Energy Program

A full articulation of the ADB Clean Energy Program was issued in a memorandum dated 26 July 2011 to rationalize various initiatives from REACH in 2001, PREGA in 2002, CEFPF in 2007, and Energy for All Initiative in 2008, in one program to achieve coherence, structure, and an organized approach in the implementation of the Clean Energy Program in ADB.

The ADB Clean Energy Program aims to lower energy-related emissions, extend supply of modern energy services to all, and improve economy-wide energy efficiency to effectively reduce the rate of growth of energy demand. All these objectives will help ADB DMCs attain energy security.

Among the activities that ADB will implement under the program are (i) expansion of clean energy investments in DMCs; (ii) implementation of demand-side clean energy components in ADB-funded projects in water, transport, urban, and agriculture sectors; and (iii) monitoring of the pipeline of clean energy projects and achievements against the outcome indicators of the 2009 Energy Policy. The scope of the Clean Energy Program includes energy efficiency, renewable energy, energy access, carbon financing, climate technology deployment, and policy and regulatory development. All these areas are meant to reinforce each other and propel ADB DMCs to a low-carbon growth path.

The approaches and phases of work identified in the articulation of the program include introducing innovations, which had started from 2008 to 2011 through various initiatives; mainstreaming and replicating proven technologies to achieve greater scale and lower costs; sharing of knowledge to sustain and continuously build on the learning and experience from implementing projects, technology exchange, and other ways; enlisting donor support to sustain the CEFPF that leverages ADB clean energy investments; and establishing partnerships in terms of knowledge and technological development. The program will use all instruments at ADB's disposal—clean energy investments, TA projects, and various loan modalities. Internally, ADB will develop its capacity in parallel with the implementation of the program including knowledge creation and sharing through various forms and venues, and building the sector and technical capacity of its staff. The following section outlines the different initiatives that help propel the Clean Energy Program with respect to energy efficiency and renewable energy, percolating low-carbon technology, financial leveraging of clean energy projects, and knowledge production and management.

4.1. Asia Solar Energy Initiative

In 2010, ADB launched the Asia Solar Energy Initiative (ASEI), whose main objective was to create a cycle of solar investments in the region that will help achieve grid parity, so that ADB DMCs optimally benefit from solar energy. It aimed to help identify, develop, and implement 3,000 MW of solar power through 2013.

Among the activities supported by ASEI was the Asia Solar Energy Forum (ASEF), which was established as a nonprofit regional knowledge management platform organization that aims to bridge the information gap between suppliers and developers in the public and private sectors and support the growth of local solar energy competence in the developing countries of Asia and the Pacific. It focuses on addressing the barriers to the application of solar and other relevant technologies such as energy storage systems and smart grids.

To demonstrate the viability of solar PV, enhance its expertise in project development, and to test a suitable business model, ADB installed a 567-kilowatt (kW) capacity solar PV power project on the roof of the ADB headquarters in Manila in 2012. Since then, ADB has supported a number of solar projects in Bangladesh, the Cook Islands, the Federated States of Micronesia, India, Maldives, Nepal, the PRC, the Philippines, Samoa, Solomon Islands, Sri Lanka, Thailand, Tonga, Uzbekistan, and Vanuatu. The targets set by the ASEI were fully achieved in 2015 when total investments amounted to $1.9 billion, catalyzing a total of 3,022.8 MW, exceeding its target of 3,000 MW. A list of the projects supported under ASEI during 2010–2015 is in Appendix 3.

4.2. Carbon Capture and Storage

Carbon capture and storage (CCS) is a technology that captures carbon dioxide (CO_2) emissions produced from the use of fossil fuels in electricity generation and industrial processes, preventing the emissions from entering the atmosphere. Since it can significantly reduce CO_2 emission, it is considered a key option among the approaches required to reduce GHG. In 2009, the Carbon Capture and Storage Fund (CCSF) was established to accelerate the physical deployment of CCS demonstration projects by promoting projects, engaging in capacity development, supporting geological investigations and environmental studies related to potential CO_2 storage sites, and undertaking community awareness and support program.[14] Priority countries for CCS assistance include India, Indonesia, the PRC, and Viet Nam. As of June 2018, the CCSF has supported 12 CCS TA projects. A preparatory TA project was approved in 2016 to assess the viability of a potential carbon capture, utilization, and storage application in the natural gas processing sector in Indonesia.

4.3. Quantum Leap in Wind

Through a TA project approved in 2011, the Quantum Leap in Wind Initiative was implemented to provide access to clean and affordable energy to more than 5 million people with additional 1 gigawatt (GW) of wind power installation in Asia excluding India and the PRC.[15] TA resources were used to implement and demonstrate the initiative in priority countries—Mongolia, the Philippines, and Sri Lanka—as they have large untapped wind power potential based on an initial assessment.

The TA project was completed in April 2017, accomplishing its goals of providing knowledge to government, private developers, utilities, regulatory commissions, and others on all aspects of wind power development. Mongolia now has 100 MW wind capacity from 0 MW. The Philippines increased its wind capacity from 33 MW to over 400 MW, and Sri Lanka from 60 MW to over 100 MW.

---

[14] ADB. *Carbon Capture Storage and Fund.* https://www.adb.org/site/funds/funds/carbon-capture-storage-fund.
[15] ADB. 2011. *Regional Technical Assistance for Quantum Leap in Wind Power Development in Asia and the Pacific.* Manila. https://www.adb.org/projects/44489-012/main#project-pds.

4.4 Small Wind Initiative

A TA project approved in 2009 supported the Small Wind Initiative to supply reliable and affordable emission-free electricity to poor communities in remote windy areas at no fuel costs.[16] Indigenous renewable energy sources were assessed in five pilot DMCs namely, Maldives, Nepal, Pakistan, Sri Lanka, and Tajikistan to supply off-grid electricity and help improve the living standards of poor and remote communities.

The pilot project in Nepal was completed and handed over to the government in June 2014. The project consisted of two sets of 5 kW wind turbines complemented by 2 kW of solar panels to meet the power demand of 43.6 kilowatt-hours (kWh) per day of 46 households in Dhaubadi.

4.5 Energy for All Initiative

In 2008, ADB embarked on the Energy for All Initiative (E4All) to empower the region's poor by providing access to energy.[17] The initiative aims to increase ADB's investment in access to energy by (i) developing new technologies and approaches to support ADB operations departments to identify, design, implement, and monitor access to energy projects; (ii) engaging in policy dialogue; and (iii) building capacity, and sharing knowledge. As part of the initiative, the Energy for All Partnership was established to serve as a platform for collaboration between ADB, governments, civil society, and the private sector to (i) promote exchange of knowledge, ideas, and information; (ii) replicate and scale up proven approaches; and (iii) build partnerships to develop, finance, and implement access to energy projects.

Through a regional TA project, E4All expanded its work to include piloting of mini- and micro-grid and other decentralized energy systems, the establishment of a Project Development Facility (PDF) and support to ADB operations departments in developing large-scale energy access projects.[18] The PDF supported energy access enterprises in developing business plans, preparing projects, and connecting with investors. The regional TA project attracted funding from bilateral sources such as the governments of Australia, Austria, Denmark, Norway, and Switzerland, and became a recognized player in the global scene.

E4All helped substantially increase ADB's investment in energy access projects. Pilot projects that were implemented in different DMCs demonstrated the viability of different business models using innovative technical and financial mechanisms to reach poor households that have limited or no access to energy. E4All was also able to lay the foundations of the PDF, which built relationships with social enterprises working on energy access. Through its knowledge-sharing and outreach activities, E4All has raised awareness within ADB and with external stakeholders on the issues and problems of energy poverty in Asia and the Pacific. Its capacity-building measures for governments and the private sector have set the foundation for the development of conducive energy access policies and the development of sustainable projects. With its efforts in energy access in the region, ADB is host to the Asia Pacific Regional Hub for SEforAll, along with UNESCAP and UNDP.

---

[16] ADB. 2009. *Regional Technical Assistance for the Effective Deployment of Distributed Small Wind Power Systems in Asian Rural Areas.* Manila. https://www.adb.org/projects/43458-012/main#project-pds.
[17] ADB. 2008. *Regional Technical Assistance for the Energy for All Initiative.* Manila. https://www.adb.org/projects/40629-012/main#project-pds.
[18] ADB. 2010. *Regional Technical Assistance for Empowering the Poor through Increasing Access to Energy.* Manila. https://www.adb.org/projects/43385-022/main#project-pds.

4.6 Asia Energy Efficiency Accelerator

ADB approved regional TA 8483 in October 2013 for $2.5 million for Asia Energy Efficiency Accelerator to increase the adoption of and investment in demand-side energy efficiency (DSEE) in ADB DMCs by creating an enabling DMC environment for increased investment in energy efficiency, initiating projects that can be replicated, and strengthening regional DSEE knowledge networks. The TA project supported knowledge and technology exchange such as the ACEF in 2015 and 2016, and knowledge and capacity building in Bangladesh, Kazakhstan, the Republic of Korea, Maldives, and the Philippines. Institutional and policy development for energy efficiency was implemented in Indonesia, Mongolia, and Sri Lanka. Activities ranged from assessing markets for the creation of energy service companies, scaling up efficient street lighting, developing energy efficiency databases, energy efficiency standards for buildings, and standards and labeling in Indonesia; conducting energy audits of buildings in Sri Lanka; and assessing the potential of DSEE in Mongolia.

The Asia Energy Efficiency Accelerator TA project strengthened knowledge and financing partnerships to enhance ADB's relevance and effectiveness in DMCs by bringing in technology solutions for energy efficiency. This project resulted in another TA project, approved in 2016, to develop energy efficiency project pipelines in DMCs in South Asia.

4.7 Low-Carbon Technology Exchange

The 16th Conference of the Parties to the UNFCCC held in 2010 reached an agreement to create a Technology Executive Committee and a Climate Technology Center and Network. To contribute to this global effort, ADB approved regional cluster TA 0008 for the Establishment of a Pilot Center to Facilitate Climate Technology Investments in Asia and the Pacific. The initiative aims to enhance the diffusion of technologies that promote low carbon and climate-resilient development in Asia and the Pacific.

Part of this TA project is the demonstration of an assisted broker model for the transfer of low-carbon technologies (LCTs) to the region. With at least two pre-selected LCTs, the project sought to prepare the necessary operational documentation for a full-fledged business based on the assisted broker model. Experts were tapped for the TA subprojects, expecting that a successful marketplace for LCT transfer to developing Asian countries would play an important role in the global climate change effort as well as help stimulate and accelerate economic development in the region.

The TA project completed the pilot business model, operational plan and procedures, and team structures in July 2015. Potential matchmaking opportunities were screened during the demonstration stage, and potential matches between providers and adopters of energy efficiency, energy storage, solar, waste-to-energy, pollution control and water technologies that focus on industry, solid waste management, grid-connected and off-grid, commercial, infrastructure, and water sectors were pursued. Toward the transfer of LCTs, the TA project offered wrap-around deal facilitation services that included (i) market development and entry strategies; (ii) technical, legal, and financial due diligence; (iii) contract drafting and negotiation support; (iv) fundraising and project financing; and (v) advisory on business opportunities.

The TA project that produced several deliverables (i) expanded business development activities with focus on India, Indonesia, the PRC, and the Philippines, and built a pipeline of potential technology transfer deals; (ii) established multiple partnerships with industry associations in the PRC, India, Singapore, and the European Union; (iii) participated in and presented at several regional events to promote its services and to reach out to

LCT stakeholders; (iv) signed a paid market entry service partnership agreement with a European technology provider of smart light-emitting diode (LED) street lighting system for expansion to India, Indonesia, and Singapore; (v) signed a paid advisory service contract with a technology adopter—an India-based water projects developer—for technology identification and deal facilitation; (vi) signed a paid advisory service contract with a Singapore-based wastewater treatment system provider who seeks to deploy its technologies in India; and (vii) brokered a commercial technology deployment agreement between a project developer in India and a Singapore-based technology provider.

4.8 Asia Climate Change and Clean Energy Venture Capital Initiative

This initiative seeks to accelerate private sector-based innovation, as well as transfer and diffuse climate change mitigation and adaptation technologies. This is done by providing equity to several venture capital funds and offering valuable technical support to fund managers to catalyze greater venture capital investment.[19]

In line with the initiative, ADB approved in April 2011 equity investments in climate technology venture capital funds of (i) up to $20 million in Aloe Environmental Fund III (Aloe Fund), (ii) up to $20 million in Keytone Ventures II (Keytone Fund) in the PRC, and (iii) up to $20 million in VenturEast Life Fund III (VenturEast Fund) in India. In August 2014, ADB, Orix Corporation, and Robeco Institutional Asset Management B.V. announced the formation of Asia Climate Partners, which would undertake commercially oriented private equity investments across a variety of environmentally supportive, low-carbon transactions throughout Asia. The Asia Climate Partners—based in Hong Kong, China—will be catalyzed initially by $400 million from its founding partners. This effort aims to provide an innovative platform to deploy capital into climate-related transactions across Asia.

The CCS TA project has been ongoing since 2019, while three of the other TA projects supporting these initiatives are in the process of being financially closed (Asia Climate Change and Clean Energy Venture Capital Initiative, Low-Carbon Technology Exchange, Small Wind Initiative). The TA projects that supported the rest of the initiatives have been physically and financially closed and rated *successful* to *highly successful*.

4.9 Leveraging Clean Energy Development

Clean Energy Financing Partnership Facility

ADB established several trust funds to support capacity building, institutional development, and project development activities in the areas of clean energy. These attracted donor contributions and led to the creation of a number of clean energy funds and the establishment of CEFPF. The CEFPF was established on 24 April 2007 to help DMCs improve energy security and transition to low-carbon use through cost-effective investments, particularly in technologies that result in GHG mitigation. CEPFP is composed of (i) the Clean Energy Fund (CEF) supported by the governments of Australia, Norway, Spain, Sweden, and the United Kingdom; (ii) the Asian Clean Energy Fund supported by the Government of Japan; (iii) the CCSF supported by the Global Carbon Capture

---

[19] ADB. 2011. *Regional Technical Assistance in Establishing a Pilot Center to Facilitate Climate Technology Investments in Asia and the Pacific - Promotion of Investment in Climate Technology Products through Venture Capital Funds.* Manila. https://www.adb.org/projects/45134-004/main#project-pds. TA 8018 is a subproject of regional cluster TA 0008.

and Storage Institute and the United Kingdom; and (iv) the Canadian Climate Fund for the Private Sector in Asia (CFPS) from the Government of Canada.

As of 31 December 2018, CEFPF's cumulative project allocations to clean energy projects have amounted to $261.1 million, supporting 190 projects. The projects are expected to contribute to about 10.3 TWh equivalent of energy savings per year, 1,567.8 MW installed capacity of renewable energy, 5.3 TWh of renewable energy generation per year, and 23.5 million tons of carbon dioxide equivalent (tCO_2) emission reduction per year. Further, the availability of concessional financing through CFPS, which was established in 2014, provided a new dimension to CEFPF and helped increase private sector investments.

4.10 Knowledge Sharing and Partnerships

Knowledge solutions and partnerships were identified in Strategy 2020 as two key drivers of change. They underpin development effectiveness and increase the relevance of ADB vis-à-vis its DMCs and development partners. ADB has organized a number of knowledge-sharing events through partnerships, of which key events are discussed below.

Asia Clean Energy Forum

Over the past 10 years, ADB's annual flagship event, the ACEF, has progressively served as the premier knowledge-sharing platform for learning and exchange of experiences on key issues and latest developments in clean energy. Since 2006, ACEF has been held annually as a week-long event in June at the ADB headquarters in Manila. It features pre-forum events and the main ACEF Forum, with an average of between 500 to 1,000 participants from over 50 countries. ACEF provides a unique platform for government officials, private sector stakeholders, technical experts, financing institutions, and civil society organizations to gather together to share experiences, knowledge, and best practices in clean energy. It has been supported by several multilateral and bilateral development partners and international organizations including the United States Agency for International Development (USAID), the United Nations Environment Programme, and Deutsche Gesellschaft für Internationale Zusammenarbeit (GIZ), Korea Energy Agency (KEA), the World Energy Council (WEC), IEA, the International Renewable Energy Agency (IRENA), the Renewable Energy Policy Network for the 21st Century (REN21), and the World Resource Institute.

Asia Solar Energy Forum

Nine knowledge-sharing ASEF events were held in all major solar markets of India, Japan, the PRC, the Philippines, the Republic of Korea, Thailand, and Uzbekistan.[20] All ASEF meetings have been supported by the host countries and attended by high-ranking government officials of the countries in the Asia and Pacific region. Among the topics discussed during the forums include the potential for solar energy development in Asia and the Pacific; applicable technologies such as PV, concentrating solar power, and smart grids; market trends; technology updates; financial approaches; policy and regulatory instruments; business models; and ways to help reduce poverty.

---

[20] Supported by ADB. 2010. *Regional Technical Assistance for the Knowledge Platform Development for the Asia Solar Energy Initiative.* Manila. https://www.adb.org/projects/44233-012/main#project-pds.

External Knowledge Partnerships

In 2011, the Guidelines for Knowledge Partnerships were issued to help set up a framework that would enable ADB to strengthen its existing knowledge partnerships and develop new ones. In line with these guidelines, ADB strengthened external partnerships with centers of excellence, international organizations, and governments. Among ADB's external partner organizations are Global Green Growth Institute (GGGI), IRENA, KEA, New Energy and Industrial Technology Development Organization (NEDO), Sustainable Energy Association of Singapore (SEAS), USAID, and WEC.

Internal Knowledge-Sharing Events and External Training

ADB's Knowledge Management Framework and its Action Plan were developed in 2009, focusing on empowering the then COPs[21] as the heart and soul of knowledge generation, incubation, and sharing in ADB. The Energy Sector Group (formerly Energy Community of Practice) has been at the center of internal knowledge-sharing events as organizers. These events focused on low-carbon clean energy technologies, business models, and financing mechanisms in the form of (i) brownbag sessions inviting external experts and technologies providers and ADB staff; and (ii) joint forums, workshops, and seminars with international organizations and centers of excellence. On average, about 15–20 brownbag sessions and 4–5 internal sector and/or thematic seminars have been organized each year to update on the latest trends in technology and knowledge in the energy sector. Other knowledge-sharing activities have also been organized to provide ADB staff an opportunity to impart to other staff members the knowledge that they acquire from external learning events such as seminars, workshops, and conferences. This served as a platform for staff to present research results, which they have conducted in the course of their work, as well as a means to generate constructive inputs and insights that could further refine their research.

---

[21] The COPs have been restructured into Sector Groups in 2015.

5 The ADB Clean Energy Program, 2008–2018

Clean Energy Investment Targets and Monitoring Methodology. Before 2008, ADB set the target for clean energy investments at $1 billion annually. This was met in the same year, with the $1.75 billion investments in clean energy from energy and other sectors. When the new Energy Policy was approved in 2009, the target was increased to $2 billion annually, to be achieved by 2013. ADB again achieved this and more, investing $2.36 billion in 2013. In 2015, following the aggressive climate goals set forth during COP21 in 2014, ADB announced that it will invest $6 billion in climate finance by 2030, $3 billion of which will be coming from mitigation investments from the energy sector. This brought slight changes in ADB's methodology of counting clean energy investments as it needed to align its own methodology with that of the multilateral development banks' (MDB) Technical Working Group on Climate Finance, where clean energy investments financed climate mitigation. Table 3 summarizes and compares both methodologies.

Table 3. Clean Energy and Climate Finance Monitoring Methodologies, Scope, and Application

	Clean Energy Investments	Climate Finance
Period	Up to 2015	From 2016
Governing Procedure	Manual for Calculating Energy Output Indicators, February 2011	Guidance Note on Counting Climate Finance in Energy, January 2017
Guidance Base	ADB Methodology	ADB Methodology based on the Joint MDB Approach
Scope and Coverage	• Clean energy components of energy and non-energy projects • Energy efficiency • Renewable energy • Fuel switching • ADB resources (Asian Development Fund, concessional ordinary capital resources lending, and ordinary capital resources) • Cofinancing administered by ADB	• Energy sector operations • Climate adaptation and mitigation activities • Fuel switching • ADB resources (Asian Development Fund, concessional ordinary capital resources lending, and ordinary capital resources) only
Exclusions	• Projects that will not bring about reduction of greenhouse gas emissions	• Greenfield fossil fuel-based power generation including gas-fired power projects

ADB = Asian Development Bank, MDB = multilateral development banks
Source: ADB.

Clean energy investments from 2008 to 2015 accounted for loans, grants, guarantees, and cofinancing administered by ADB that finance clean energy components of projects from energy and other sectors including agriculture and natural resources, transport, urban, and water that result in reduced GHG emissions. Fuel switching from a dirtier fossil fuel to a cleaner source such as gas is considered, as is the replacement of a dirtier or less efficient power plant with virtually a new power plant whose fuel comes from a cleaner source like gas. Such replacement to cleaner fuel, however, does not pass the climate finance methodology even if they substantially reduced GHG emissions starting 2016. And because target climate investments have been appropriated to various sectors, clean energy or climate mitigation finance monitoring from 2016 focused solely on projects under the energy sector. Of the $4 billion mitigation investments target for instance, $3 billion will be coming from energy while $1 billion will be from the transport sector. Figure 2 and the following narrative should be taken with this caveat in mind.

ADB Clean Energy Investments, 2008–2018

Three broad types are taken into consideration when categorizing clean energy investments in ADB: (i) renewable energy includes power generation using different renewable energy sources including large and small hydropower and renewable energy-dedicated transmission and distribution projects; (ii) energy efficiency investments that could either be demand-side or supply-side energy efficiency projects that bring about electricity or energy savings from meeting the same level of demand with less energy inputs; and (iii) fuel switching activities that replace more carbon-intensive fuel with cleaner alternatives (e.g., replacing diesel-fired plants with combined cycle gas turbines).

Figure 2 shows clean energy investments for the past decade in the broad categories mentioned with investments skewed toward renewable energy at an average of $1.2 billion per year. It was only in 2015 that energy efficiency projects exceeded renewable energy investments after it took 55% of total clean energy investments. ADB's total investment on energy efficiency projects was about $764 million on an annual average over the review period. Switching to cleaner fuel appears intermittently for 4 years at varying levels from 2010 to 2015 but has not figured since 2016.

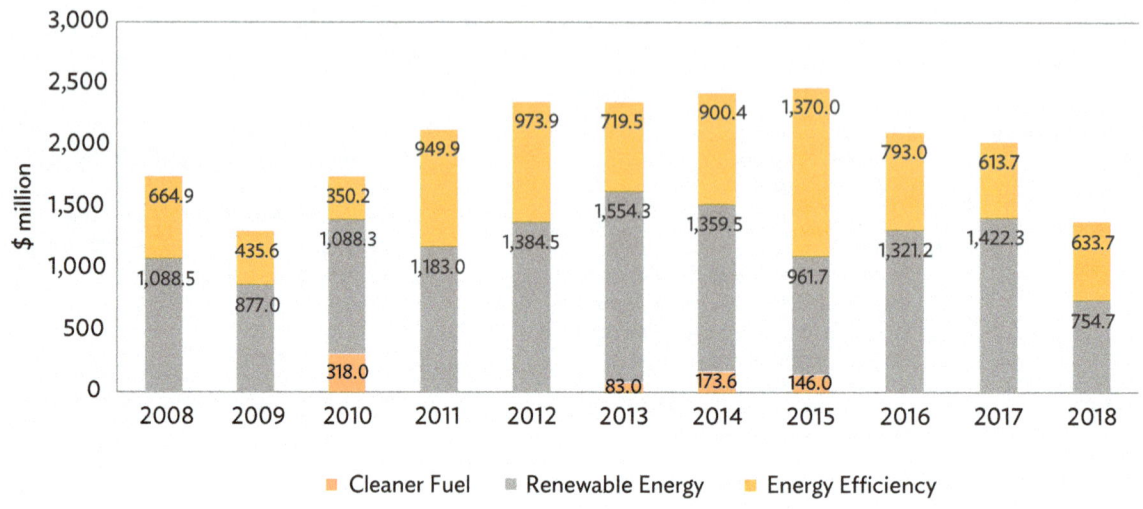

Figure 2: Clean Energy Investments by Category, 2008–2018 ($ million)

Source: ADB.

From 2008, sovereign operations invested more than nonsovereign operations on average at about $1.2 billion annually. Nonsovereign operations exceeded sovereign operations only in 2015, with 74% share of the total clean energy investments.

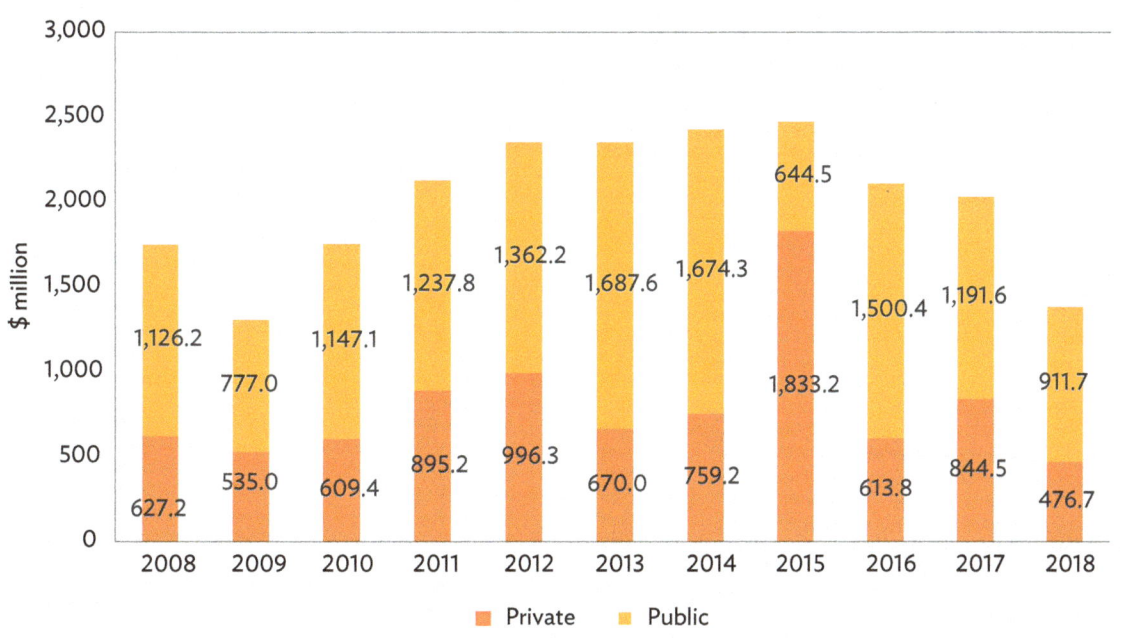

Figure 3: Clean Energy Investments by Operations, 2008–2018 ($ million)

Source: ADB.

Renewable Energy. Various renewable energy technologies were tried and tested by ADB under the Clean Energy Program from 2008 to 2018 (Figure 4). Because of its proven technology, large and small hydropower projects (including hydro-dedicated transmission and distribution lines) figured significantly from 2008 to 2014, accounting for at least 24% to a maximum of 88% of clean energy investments in the renewable energy sphere. Renewable energy generation from solar including solar power plant-dedicated transmission and distribution asserted its dominance particularly in 2016, with 58% share of total clean energy investments in renewable energy until it settled in the vicinity of 40% share for the last 2 years in 2017 and 2018. The use of biomass and waste for various energy applications showed a significant share of 34% in 2009 and 2012 before tapering off since then and picking up again in the last 3 years since 2016. Wind energy projects, like hydropower projects, figure consistently every year at varying proportions from a low of 1% in 2012 to a high of 44% in 2010. Figure 4 shows the amounts and shares of renewable energy technologies over the review period.

Energy Efficiency. Investments in energy efficiency consist of financing for for demand-side and supply-side measures that reduce energy demand.[22] This averaged about $764 million every year during the review period. Figure 5 shows the trend of energy efficiency investment by the two categories. The demand-side investments registered from 2009 to 2015 are largely attributable to energy efficiency measures from other sectors when the scope of clean energy monitoring included clean energy components in projects from agriculture and natural resources, transport, urban, and water sectors. The DSEE invested in 2016 was for the financing of various energy efficiency projects in India such as the use of efficient household lighting replacing incandescent lights,

---

[22] Demand-side energy efficiency measures are activities that alter energy demand from the end-user side while supply-side energy efficiency measures aim to save energy from system losses avoided.

more efficient agricultural water pumps, and LED street lighting. Overall, investments in energy efficiency were characterized by sporadic gains, and investments in supply-side energy efficiency measures outweighed those for the demand-side energy efficiency in 2008-2018. Investments in later years could be traced to efficiency improvement and energy savings from cutting down system losses.

Figure 4: Clean Energy Investments by Renewable Energy Technology, 2008–2018 ($ million)

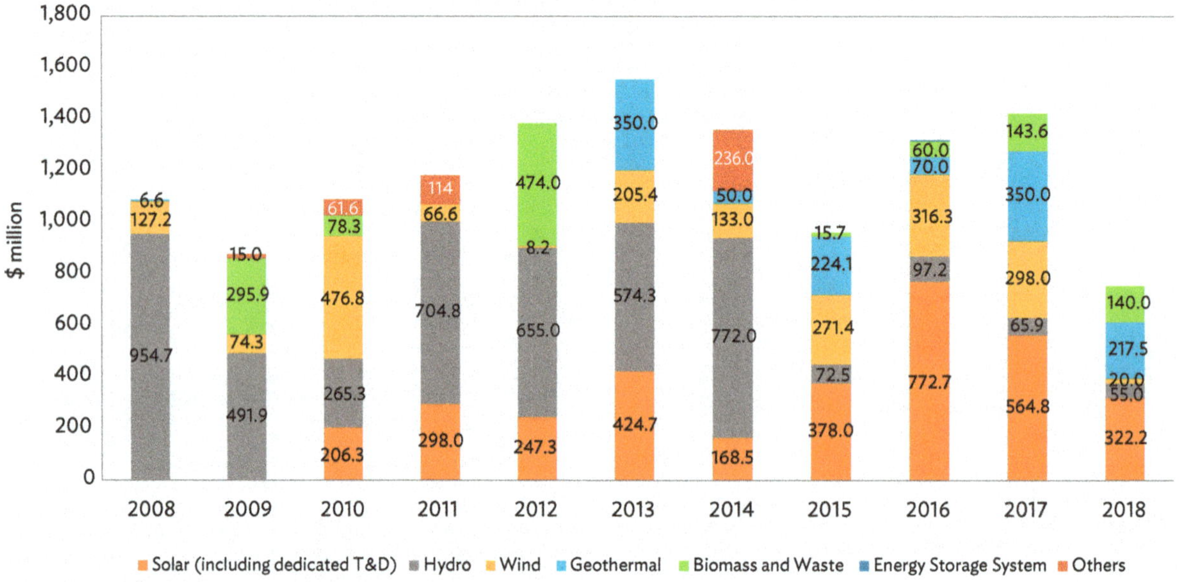

[Stacked bar chart showing investments in $ million by year 2008-2018, with categories: Solar (including dedicated T&D), Hydro, Wind, Geothermal, Biomass and Waste, Energy Storage System, Others.

2008: Hydro 954.7, Wind 127.2, Biomass and Waste 6.6
2009: Hydro 491.9, Wind 295.9, Biomass and Waste 74.3, Others 15.0
2010: Solar 206.3, Hydro 265.3, Wind 476.8, Biomass and Waste 78.3, Others 61.6
2011: Solar 298.0, Hydro 704.8, Wind 66.6, Biomass and Waste 114
2012: Solar 247.3, Hydro 655.0, Wind 8.2, Biomass and Waste 474.0
2013: Solar 424.7, Hydro 574.3, Wind 205.4, Energy Storage System 350.0
2014: Solar 168.5, Hydro 772.0, Wind 133.0, Geothermal 50.0, Energy Storage System 236.0
2015: Solar 378.0, Hydro 72.5, Wind 271.4, Energy Storage System 224.1, Others 15.7
2016: Solar 772.7, Hydro 97.2, Energy Storage System 316.3, Biomass and Waste 70.0, Others 60.0
2017: Solar 564.8, Hydro 65.9, Wind 298.0, Energy Storage System 350.0, Biomass and Waste 143.6
2018: Solar 322.2, Hydro 55.0, Wind 20.0, Energy Storage System 217.5, Biomass and Waste 140.0]

T & D = transmission and distribution.
Source: ADB.

Figure 5: Energy Efficiency Investments by Type, 2008–2018 ($ million)

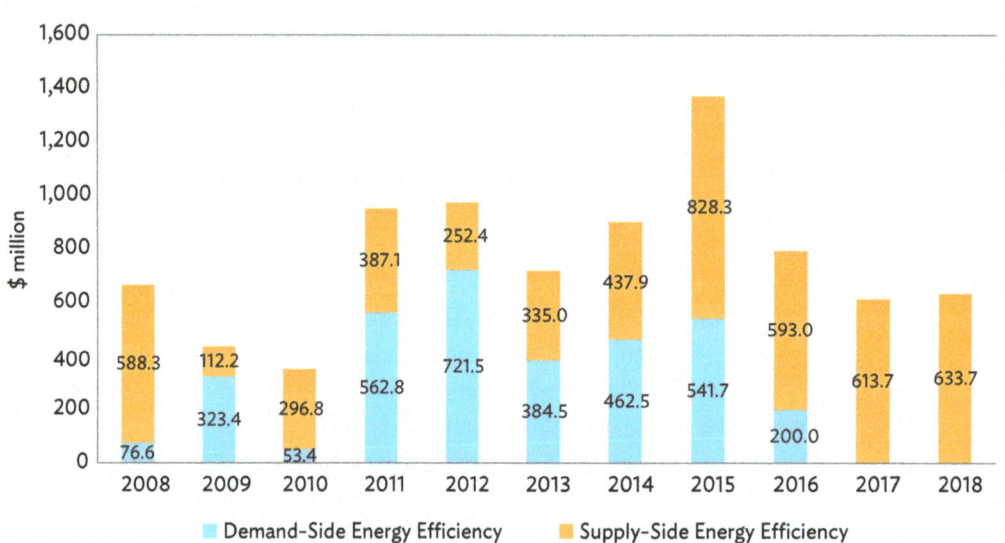

Source: ADB.

Energy Access. Before the establishment of the Energy for All Initiative in 2008, ADB had provided financing for energy access projects. Average annual investments in energy access from 2003 to 2007 was $119 million annually. The volume picked up when structure and organization to scale up energy access efforts were installed under the banner of Energy for All. Investments increased by 66% from 2007 to $476 million in 2008. Average annual investments reached about $854 million yearly from 2009 to 2018, providing improved energy access to 2.4 million households on average every year. Figure 6 shows this trend. All things equal, the variations that can be observed between the movement of investments and household connections over the review period can be explained by the difference in the costs and type of energy access projects. A district heating project was able to connect fewer households than an improvement in transmission and distribution line project at the same cost.

Figure 6: ADB Energy Access Investment ($ million) and Improved Energy Access (number of households), 2003–2018

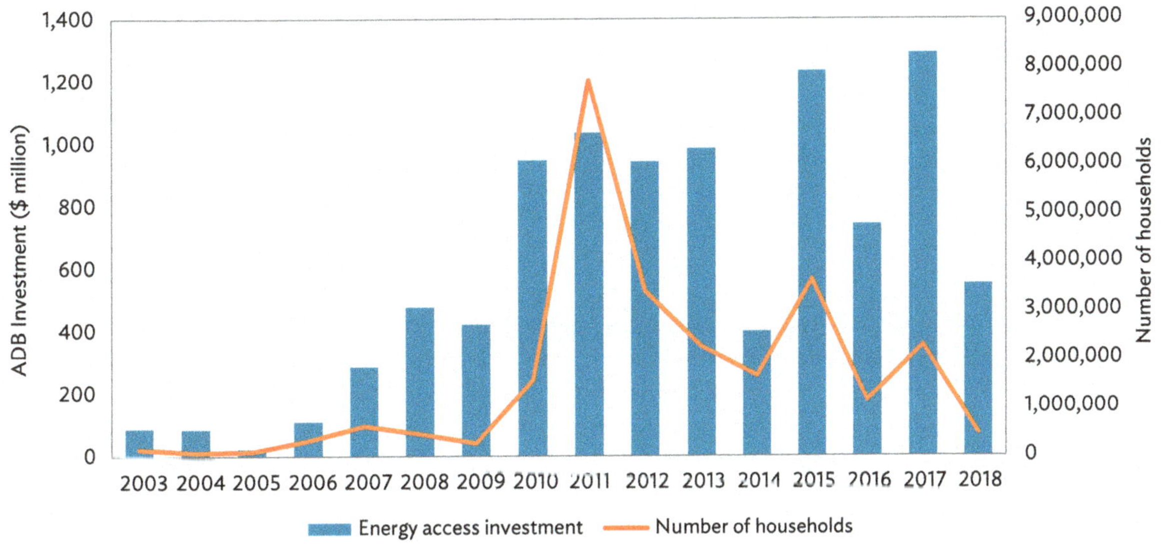

ADB = Asian Development Bank.
Source: ADB.

Energy Access by Operations. An average of $820 million every year was invested by sovereign operations in energy access, which represent almost 100% of total investments over the review period (Figure 7). Transmission has traditionally been in the public sector domain due to the natural monopoly characteristics of the subsector but electricity distribution, while deemed relatively competitive, is imbued with social and quasi-public good considerations especially when it pertains to expanding access in rural off-grid areas.

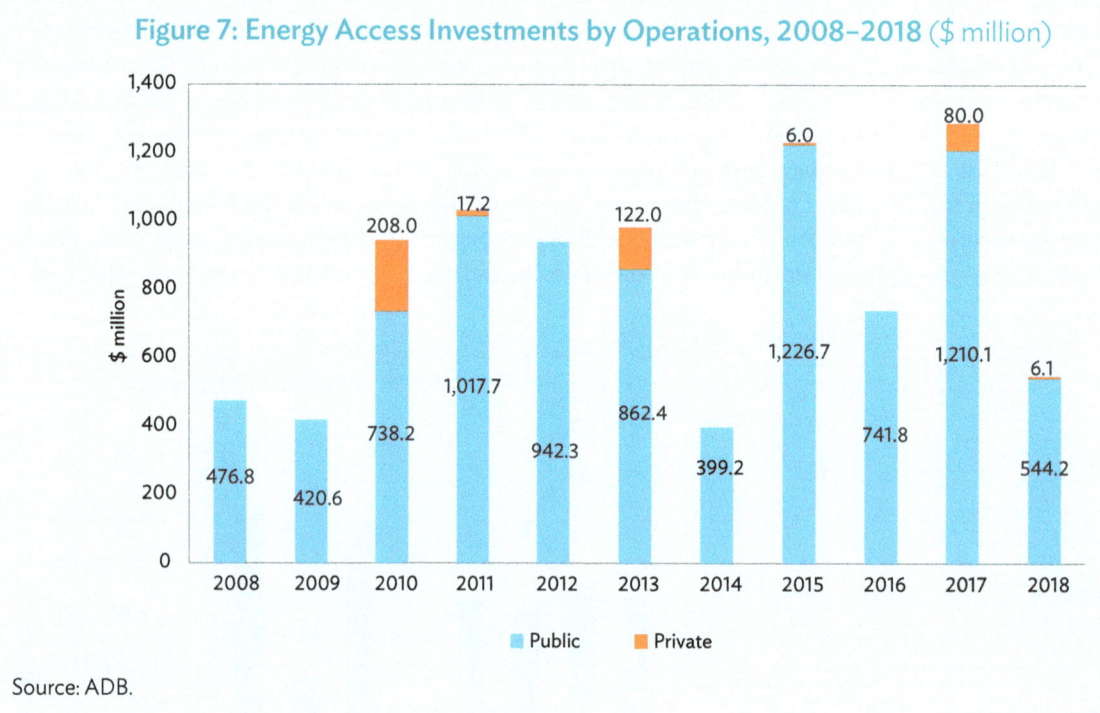

Figure 7: Energy Access Investments by Operations, 2008–2018 ($ million)

Source: ADB.

Energy Access by Category. Energy access investments can be broken down into the following categories based on type of project and their components: (i) stand-alone distribution systems improvement that aim to improve reliability and availability of electricity supply; (ii) investments in clean cooking and heating for new and improved connections of households being given these services; (iii) rural electrification, both on, and off-grid; and (iv) other projects that provide financing and guarantees for energy access or those that have varied components (Figure 8).

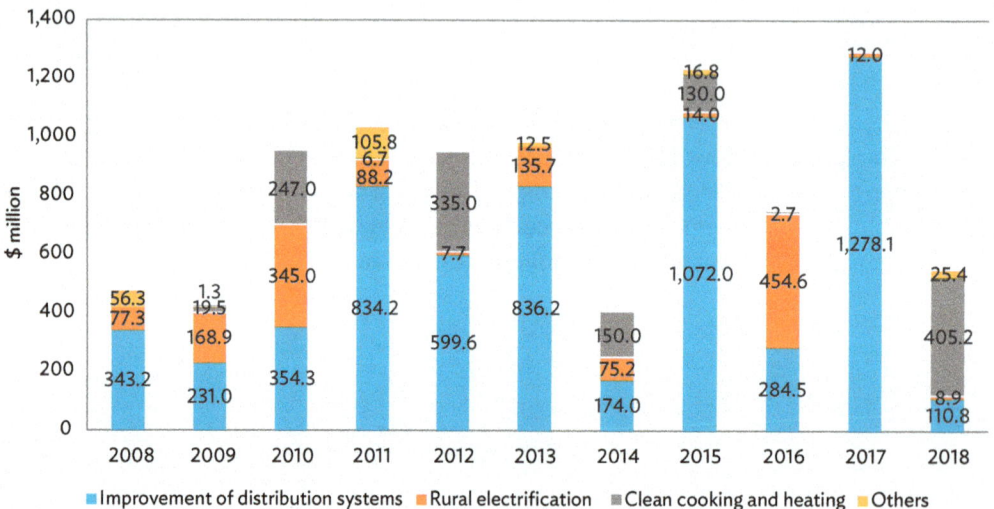

Figure 8: ADB Energy Access Investments by Category, 2008–2018 ($ million)

ADB=Asian Development Bank.
Source: ADB.

Majority of the energy access projects approved from 2008 to 2018 involved investments to improve distribution systems, which recorded an annual average of $556 million or 68% of the total energy access investments. For the same period, yearly averages show that rural and off-grid electrification accounted for 16%, and clean cooking, heating and district heating for 14%.

From 2008 to 2018, ADB invested a total of $1.3 billion in clean cooking and heating, and on improving district heating systems. An average of $19.6 million every year was used to finance access to clean cooking and heating while $98 million was invested in the improvement of district heating systems on average per year (Figure 9). Projects that provide access to clean cooking and heating included using cleaner fuel such as biogas, natural gas, and LPG and improved cooking devices such as improved biomass stoves. All district heating projects were implemented in the PRC due to the country's high demand for space heating. Interventions done in this sphere can be characterized by the use of low-carbon, low-emission, and energy-efficient district heating systems.

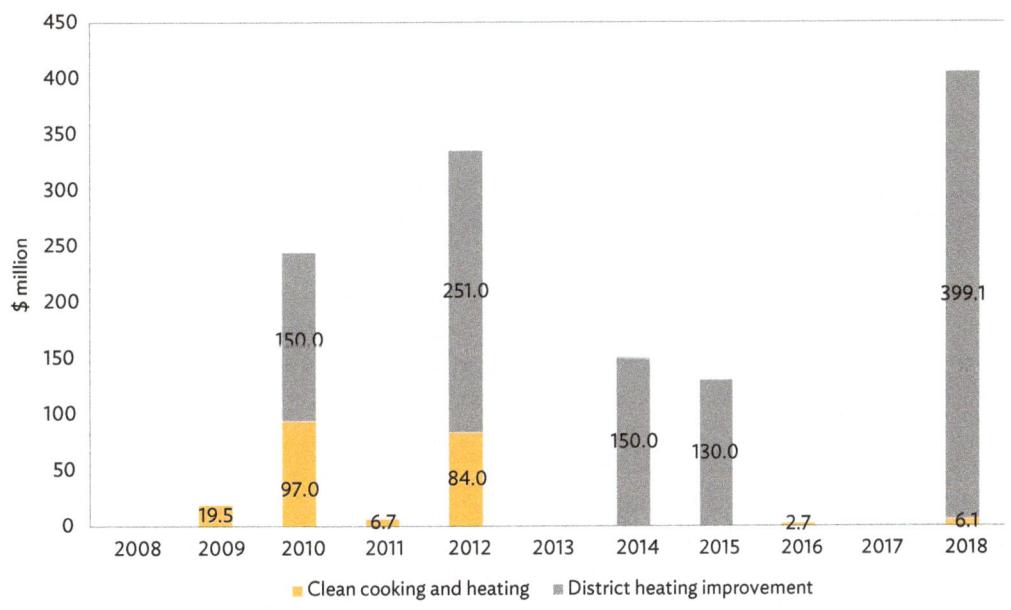

Figure 9: Energy Access Investments in Clean Cooking, Heating, and Improvement of District Heating Systems, 2008–2018 ($ million)

Source: ADB.

Investments in access to clean cooking are comparatively less and in smaller amounts compared to investments in projects that require higher capital expenditures such as new electricity connections or improvement in distribution and heating systems. Providing clean cooking, however, has larger social development impacts and co-benefits, and can be interfaced with broader social development projects such as those in health, gender, or agriculture and rural development. This should not, however, preclude any typical energy access projects along the lines of electricity connections and the like, to make access to clean cooking a component. There are after all, about 1.7 billion people in developing Asia that have no access to clean cooking, including 1.4 billion that continue to rely on traditional biomass for cooking.[23]

---

[23] International Energy Agency. 2018. *World Energy Outlook 2018. Clean Cooking and Electricity Access Databases.* https://www.iea.org/sdg/electricity/ and https://www.iea.org/sdg/cooking/. Accessed August 2018.

6 Clean Energy Program Results, 2008–2018

The Clean Energy Program results will be measured against seven indicators from the 2009 Energy Policy Results Framework: (i) more than $2 billion invested in clean energy annually from 2013; (ii) increase in additional installed capacity using renewable energy from the baseline; (iii) increase in electricity savings yearly from the baseline; (iv) increase in the reduction of CO_2 emissions from the baseline; (v) increase in the number of electricity access projects from the baseline; (vi) increase in the amount of electricity access investments from the baseline; and (vii) increase in the number of households connected to electricity from the baseline set in the 2009 Energy Policy, which is the average level of outcomes from 2005 to 2007.

ADB has reached its target of investing more than $2 billion annually in clean energy since 2013 except in 2018. The decline started in 2016 when the scope and data set of clean energy projects were changed in light of the climate finance targets that were set in 2015 and appropriated across different sectors. Clean energy investments of projects in other sectors (e.g., agriculture, transport, water, and urban) and the share of cofinancing have been excluded. On the average, however, during the review period, ADB invested just within the target of $2 billion every year. It exceeded the baseline of $0.70 billion every year of the review period.

The decline in 2017 reflects the overall decline of renewable energy generation costs in the global market, which according to IRENA has fallen significantly. From their cost database, IRENA reported in 2017 that the global weighted average costs of electricity generation from all renewables in 2016 excluding concentrated solar power (CSP) and offshore wind, went down significantly to the level of fossil fuels at $0.45/kWh to $0.14/kWh. Solar and wind power technologies are considered commercially mature and IRENA had projected for further cost reductions.[24] The cost per megawatt of typical utility-scale solar PV systems was estimated to have gone down 25% in 2017 from 2015 levels, according to Bloomberg New Energy Finance.[25] With the reduction in costs came the increase in additional capacity from renewables, growing from 2,017 GW in 2016 to 2,197 GW in 2017.[26] This trend of getting more renewable capacity for every dollar investment continued in 2018. Solar PV investment went down by 1% while wind investment was unchanged.[27] And yet, additional capacity from renewables increased by 8% to 2,378 GW in 2018.[28]

This was the global backdrop of ADB clean energy investments that went substantially below target in 2018. One case of note that is closer to home is the reduction in solar investments in the PRC that plummeted by 24% in 2018 to $130.8 billion—which according to Bloomberg New Energy Finance was due to the reduction in capital

---

[24] International Renewable Energy Agency. 2017. *Renewable Power: Sharply Falling Generation Costs.* https://www.irena.org/-/media/Files/IRENA/Agency/Publication/2017/Nov/%20IRENA_Sharply_falling_costs_2017.pdf
[25] Bloomberg New Energy Finance. 2018. *Clean Energy Investment Trends 2017.* https://data.bloomberglp.com/bnef/sites/14/2018/01/BNEF-Clean-Energy-Investment-Investment-Trends-2017.pdf
[26] Renewable Energy Policy Network for the 21st Century. 2018. *Renewables 2018: Global Status Report.* http://www.ren21.net/gsr-2018/.
[27] International Energy Agency. 2019. *World Energy Investment 2019.* https://www.iea.org/wei2019/.
[28] Renewable Energy Policy Network for the 21st Century. 2018. *Renewables 2019: Global Status Report.* https://www.ren21.net/reports/global-status-report/.

costs and a sudden change in policy in the country during the middle of the year.[29] Taken by itself, the drop was largely on account of the 47% rate of decrease in renewable energy investments where there was a drastic 93% reduction in wind energy investments from 2017 levels. Barring investments in energy storage (which appeared for the first time in 2018), all of ADB's investments in renewable energy technologies in 2018 went down at varying rates: 43% for solar, 38% for geothermal, 17% for hydropower and 3% for biomass and waste from the previous year. There were at least four renewable energy projects using various technologies with a total amount of about $133.9 million that fell from the 2018 approvals. This notwithstanding, total energy sector portfolio in 2018 decreased from about $5.5 billion in 2017 to $3.9 billion in 2018—showing substantial reduction overall. There were 29 clean energy projects approved in 2017 and only 20 in 2018. The number of renewable energy projects decreased from 18 in 2017 to 13 in 2018; and the number of projects with investments that ranged from $100 million to $199 million stayed flat while those that were below $100 million decreased by five. Figure 10 shows the trend in ADB clean energy investments compared to the baseline average and the target of $2 billion per year.

It can also be posited that since in recent years, solar PV and onshore wind have become competitive with conventional energy generation, private investors and commercial banks have become the main sources of funding, while ADB has increased its financing in electricity transmission and distribution systems that can integrate more renewable energy. The global energy investment data including clean energy from various sources (BNEF, IEA, and REN21), finds that the bulk, or 75%, of renewable energy investments in 2018 were found in Europe. Fossil fuel spending exceeded that of renewable energy in the Middle East and North Africa region and Southeast Asia. Renewable energy investments in Southeast Asia remained the same in 2018 from the previous

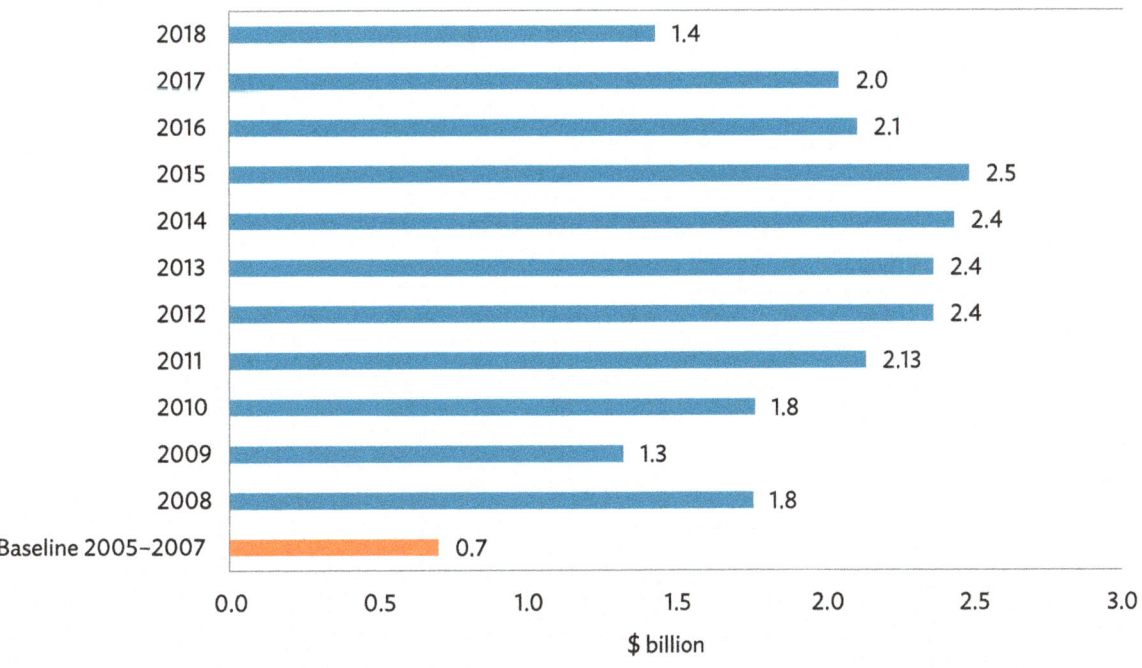

Figure 10: Clean Energy Investments, 2008–2018 ($ billion)

Source: ADB.

---

[29] Bloomberg New Energy Finance. Clean Energy Investments Exceeded $300 Billion Once Again in 2018. https://about.bnef.com/blog/clean-energy-investment-exceeded-300-billion-2018/

year with issues such as risks in grid development, financial performance of existing utilities, and poor bankability of renewable energy projects in markets like Indonesia and Viet Nam—were cited to be the main causes of the slowdown.[30] Based on these trends, it seems that in some regions, such as Southeast Asia, renewables are not the first fuel of choice; or, financing constraints have forced them to make these choices instead. These are critical issues that could also be seen in other markets in Asia and the Pacific. The combination of the technical, financial, economic, and institutional soundness and viability that should go with each investment could not be more emphasized in this regard.

Additional capacity from renewable energy sources during the review period exceeded the baseline of 500 MW (Figure 11). ADB renewable energy projects helped install more than 2 GW of additional capacity from projects approved in 2014 and 2016. Capacity largely came from large hydro projects that accounted for 35% of additional capacity added or about 713 MW, followed by wind energy projects that contributed 560 MW or 27% of total capacity added from renewable energy sources. Renewable energy projects accounted for more than half the clean energy investments made in 2014 at 55%.

In 2016, the capacity addition from renewable energy sources was largely attributed to wind and solar projects that accounted for 46% and 35%, respectively, of the total capacity. Investments in renewable energy represented 62% of overall clean energy investments in 2016.

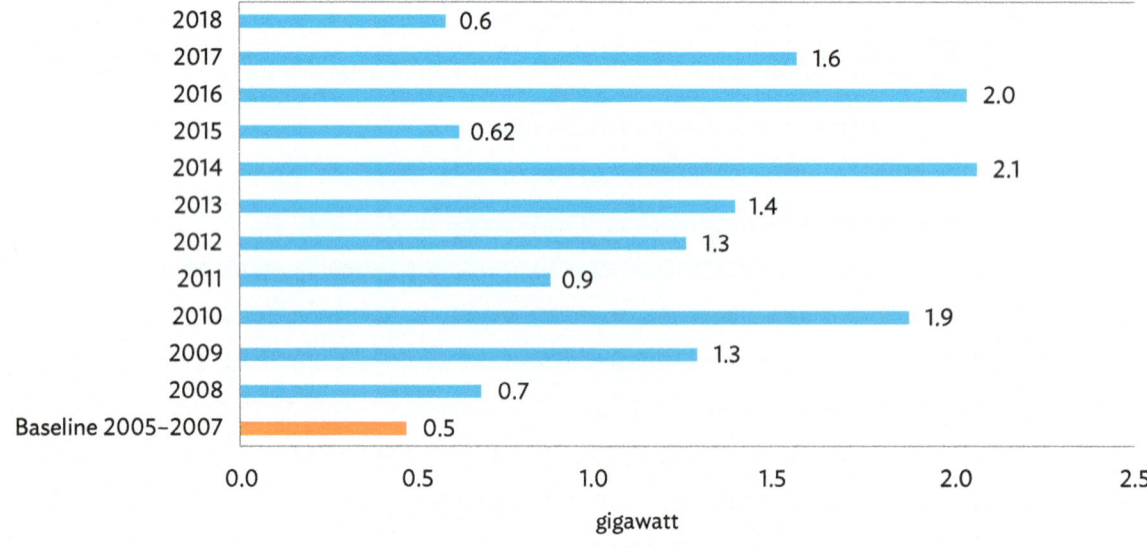

Figure 11: Additional Capacity Using Renewable Energy, 2008–2018 (gigawatt)

Source: ADB.

It was only in 2009 that electricity savings surpassed the baseline of 9.8 TWh (Figure 12). Electricity savings during this year was mainly bolstered by three projects: one demand-side energy efficiency project each in the transport sector in Pakistan and in the energy sector in the PRC, and one supply-side energy efficiency project in the energy sector in India. All three collectively were estimated to have contributed about 8 TWh of the 11 TWh per year.

---

[30] IEA. 2019.

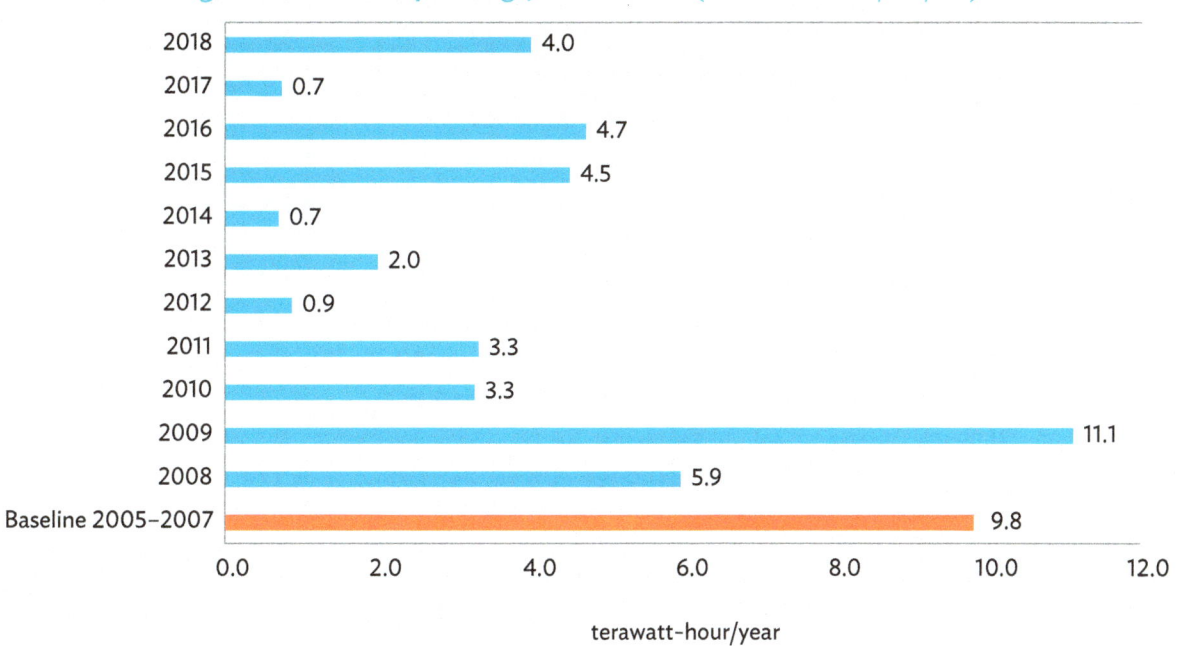

Figure 12: Electricity Savings, 2008–2018 (terawatt-hour per year)

Source: ADB.

Energy efficiency projects were fewer compared to renewable energy projects during the period in terms of number and types of projects. The projects in this sphere seem to only generate marginal electricity savings from the types of interventions implemented: electricity savings from transmission and distribution in the energy sector, and DSEE in agriculture and natural resources, transport, and water sectors. While this area requires the most effort and attention, especially when it has the greater potential to bring CO_2 emissions down, energy efficiency projects are also more complex, their implementation not as straightforward, and their outcomes are not tangible compared to those of renewable energy projects. For one, electricity savings did not seem to move in the same direction and proportionate magnitude as energy efficiency investments. Investment decreased by 26% in 2013 from the previous year but energy savings increased by 129%. In 2014, investment increased by 25% and energy savings decreased by 65%.

CO_2 emissions reduced from ADB clean energy projects exceeded the baseline for most of the years during the review period except in 2013 (Figure 13). The very low electricity savings relative to the baseline, and the relatively unchanged additional capacity using renewable energy from the previous year could have affected this low CO_2 emission reduction in 2013.

Figure 13: Carbon Dioxide Emission Reduction, 2008–2018
(million tons of CO_2-equivalent/year)

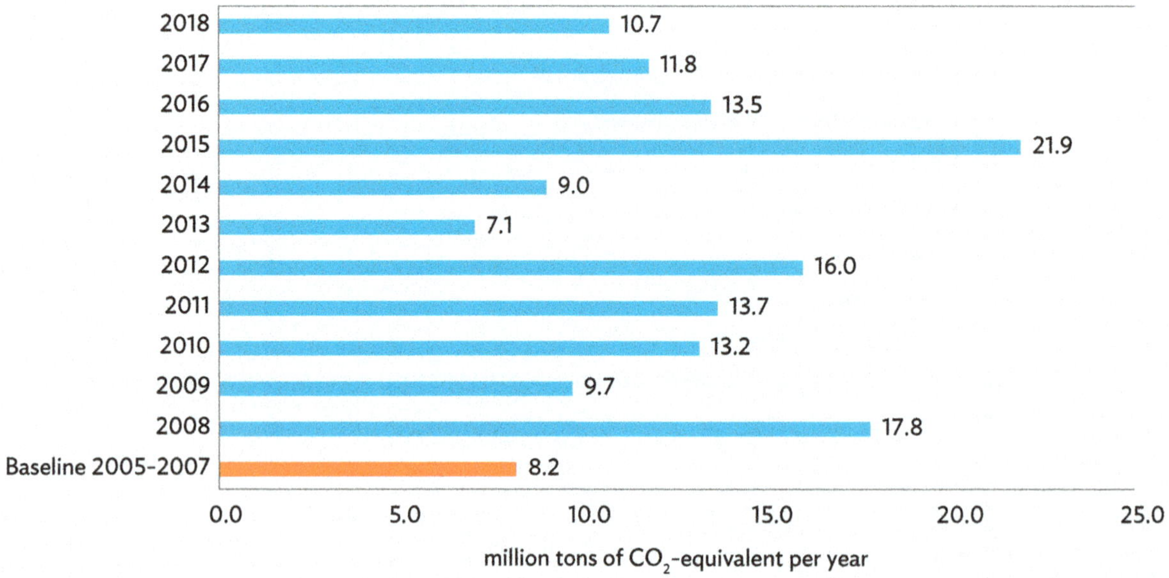

Year	million tons of CO_2-equivalent per year
2018	10.7
2017	11.8
2016	13.5
2015	21.9
2014	9.0
2013	7.1
2012	16.0
2011	13.7
2010	13.2
2009	9.7
2008	17.8
Baseline 2005–2007	8.2

Source: ADB.

There were on average four energy access projects per year from 2005 to 2007, which was surpassed every year from 2008 to 2018, with the lowest at five projects in 2017 (Figure 14). The low showing was, however compensated by the volume of investments in 2017 when it registered the highest level of energy access investments as can be seen in Figure 15.

Figure 14: Energy Access Projects, 2008–2018 (number of projects)

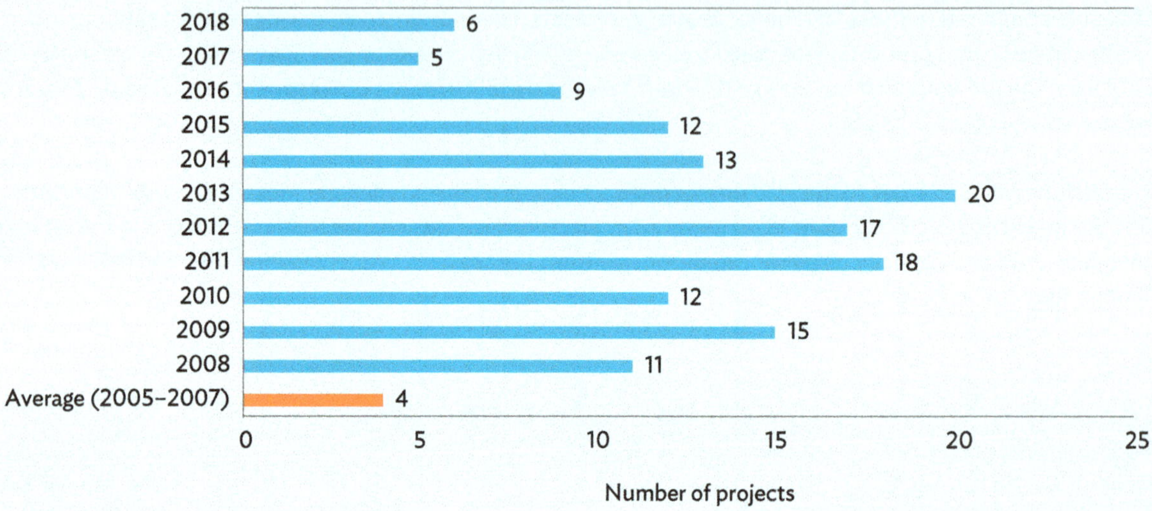

Year	Number of projects
2018	6
2017	5
2016	9
2015	12
2014	13
2013	20
2012	17
2011	18
2010	12
2009	15
2008	11
Average (2005–2007)	4

Source: ADB.

Energy access investments are shown to have consistently surpassed the baseline as seen in Figure 15. Investments were remarkable particularly in 2011, 2015, and 2017 driven as expected by activities in improving distribution systems. It should be noted that the methodology of counting for energy access investments, unlike clean energy investments, include TA projects that prepare for or facilitate energy access projects.

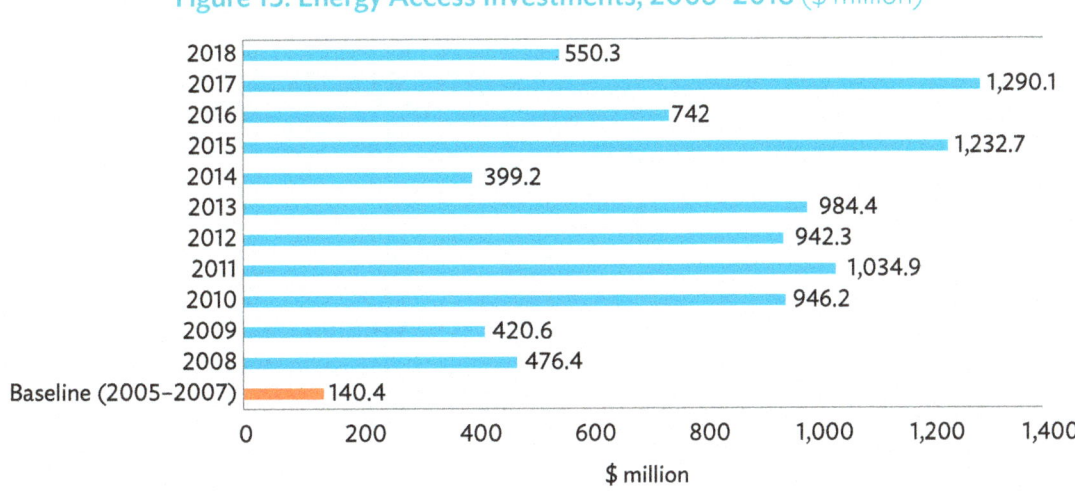

Figure 15: Energy Access Investments, 2008–2018 ($ million)

Year	$ million
2018	550.3
2017	1,290.1
2016	742
2015	1,232.7
2014	399.2
2013	984.4
2012	942.3
2011	1,034.9
2010	946.2
2009	420.6
2008	476.4
Baseline (2005–2007)	140.4

Source: ADB.

Energy access targets under the 2009 Energy Policy pertain only to new and improved electricity connections. This review will then remove energy access projects that provide clean cooking, new and improved district heating, or cooling services from the dataset, and only assess the level of achievement based on new and improved household electricity connections from the baseline. Figure 16 shows that ADB's efforts in connecting additional households to electricity and improving electricity access during the review period exceeded the baseline from 2010 to 2018, while it did not quite meet it in 2009 when rural electrification dominated the energy access projects approved during the year. Rural electrification projects are by nature smaller in terms of scale and beneficiary reach as opposed to transmission and distribution projects that are more encompassing and far reaching.

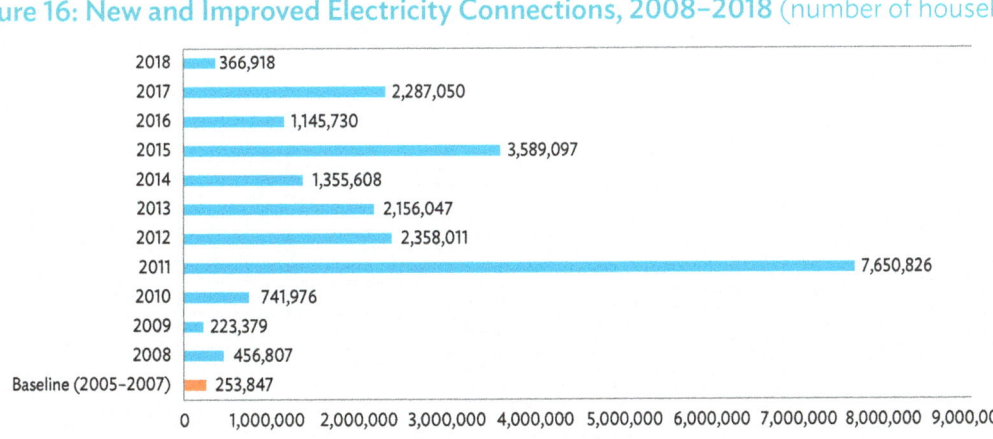

Figure 16: New and Improved Electricity Connections, 2008–2018 (number of households)

Year	Number of households
2018	366,918
2017	2,287,050
2016	1,145,730
2015	3,589,097
2014	1,355,608
2013	2,156,047
2012	2,358,011
2011	7,650,826
2010	741,976
2009	223,379
2008	456,807
Baseline (2005–2007)	253,847

Source: ADB.

In summary, of the seven indicators being assessed in this review, only the target for energy savings did not exceed the baseline with relative consistency throughout the review period compared to the other indicators (Table 4). It is the area in which ADB in the coming years would like to improve, given energy efficiency's high impact potential in making a significant dent on reducing CO_2 emissions, and enhancing energy security, power system resilience, and sustainability.

Table 4. Summary of Clean Energy Program Achievements by Energy Policy Results Framework Indicator

Target (Baseline 2005–2007)	ADB Sector Accomplishments
Promoting energy efficient and renewable energy	
Amount of investment – $2 billion per year from 2013	The target was achieved from 2008 to 2017. Clean energy investments surpassed the baseline annually from 2008 to 2018, with the average annual investment at $2.01 billion.
Additional renewable energy installed capacity – increased from baseline	The 2005–2007 baseline average was exceeded every year from 2008 to 2018, averaging 1.29 GW of renewable energy capacity installed per year.
Electricity saved per year – increased from baseline	Average annual electricity savings during the review period was 3.73 terawatt-hours (TWh) per year per year. The 2005–2007 baseline of 9.8 TWh per year was surpassed only in 2009.
Amount of CO_2 emission reduction – increased from baseline	The 2005–2007 baseline of 8.20 million tons of carbon dioxide (tCO_2)-equivalent per year was exceeded yearly during the review period except in 2013. Average carbon dioxide emission reduction per year from 2008 to 2018 is 13.11 million tCO_2-equivalent annually.
Maximizing access to energy for all	
Number of loans and grants – increased from baseline	The 2005–2007 baseline of four energy access projects per year was surpassed every year throughout the review period.
Amount of investment in energy access – increased from baseline	The baseline of $140.45 million of investments in energy access was surpassed consistently every year during the review period reaching a record high of $1.3 billion in 2017.
New households connected to electricity – increased from baseline	The annual total number of new and improved household electricity connections from 2008 to 2018 surpassed the baseline of 253,847 households, except in 2009. The highest number of households given new and improved electricity connections was 7.6 million in 2011.

Source: ADB.

7 Findings and Conclusion

Formally instituted in 2011, the ADB Clean Energy Program has played two important roles. First, it consolidated ADB's initiatives in renewable energy, energy efficiency, and energy access with the aims of promoting deployment of renewable energy, improving economy-wide energy efficiency to effectively reduce the energy demand, and extending the supply of modern energy services to all. Second, it anticipated and institutionalized the necessary responses to reduce energy-related greenhouse gas emissions through innovative technologies. The objectives of the Clean Energy Program are aligned with the global commitments set in 2015 when the United Nations included energy as part of the 2030 Agenda for Sustainable Development,[31] and the Paris Agreement provided the impetus for all nations to combat climate change and pursue a sustainable low-carbon future.[32]

ADB investments on clean energy focused on cleaner fuel, energy efficiency, and renewable energy. The output indicators set on the 2009 Energy Policy Results Framework were used to assess the achievements and performance of the Clean Energy Program from 2008 to 2018 against the 2005–2007 baseline. The said indicators give a preview of the projects' performance in terms of renewable energy, energy efficiency, and energy access.[33] A total of 384 clean energy projects were reviewed for this report.

Overall, the Clean Energy Program achieved the target of investing $2 billion annually in clean energy starting 2013, as indicated in the ADB Energy Policy 2009.[34] Total clean energy investment in 2018 was about $1.4 billion. This was due to the declining cost of renewable energy, and the maturity of the renewable markets with increasing commercial financing. At the same time, ADB increased its financing on transmission and distribution networks that are needed to integrate more renewable energy. Annual investment in clean energy averaged $2.01 billion annually from 2008 to 2018, which is higher than the $700 million baseline.[35] Cumulative investments in clean energy amounted to $22.12 billion for the said period.

Renewable energy. Investments in renewable energy had the biggest share at 58.7% of the total investments in clean energy for 2008 to 2018, while energy efficiency had 38.0% and cleaner fuel 3.3%. Cumulative investments in renewable energy amounted to about $12.99 trillion from 2008 to 2018. Hydro had the largest share at 36.2% of the total renewable energy investment for 2008 to 2018. Solar, which comprised many small-scale projects, followed closely with 26.0%, then wind at 15.4%, biomass and waste at 9.7%, and geothermal at 9.3%. The additional renewable energy capacity averaged 1.29 GW annually in the same period, which is almost triple the

---

[31] SDG 7 advocates access to affordable, reliable, sustainable, and modern energy for all, while SDG 13 calls for urgent action to combat climate change and its impacts.
[32] Through the Nationally Determined Contributions, the Paris Agreement has contracted the nations to strengthen the global response to the threat of climate change.
[33] Refer to Table 2 for the indicators.
[34] ADB achieved the $2 billion annual target to invest in clean energy ahead of schedule. ADB had been investing more than $2 billion since 2011, and in that particular year, it invested a total of $2.13 billion in clean energy.
[35] Review period is 2008 to 2018, and baseline is computed using data from 2005 to 2007.

baseline of 0.47 GW. Cumulative installation of additional renewable energy capacity reached 14.22 GW from 2008 to 2018.

Energy efficiency. Investments in energy efficiency resulted in average annual energy savings of 3.73 terawatt-hours (TWh) for 2008 to 2018, which is only about a third of the 9.8 TWh baseline. This 2005 to 2007 baseline is a high standard as the Energy Efficiency Initiative was launched in 2005, resulting in an abundance of energy efficiency projects around this time. Both demand- and supply-side energy efficiency measures over the review period showed sporadic gains.

Cumulative investments in energy efficiency amounted to about $8.40 billion from 2008 to 2018. Investments in supply-side energy efficiency was almost double (60.4% of the total energy efficiency investment) that of demand-side energy efficiency (39.6%) for 2008 to 2018. Supply-side measures that reduce system losses made up majority of ADB's portfolio on energy efficiency. ADB also undertook projects that replaced incandescent lights, and used more efficient water pumps and LED street lighting. In earlier years, ADB invested in demand-side energy efficiency measures in other sectors such as agriculture, natural resources, transport, urban, and water, which were previously counted as clean energy projects, until the change in 2016.

Energy access. Universal access to affordable energy is a prerequisite to inclusive growth. Indicators of ADB's investments in energy access, which focused on access to electricity, have had good outcomes on long-running programs such as ADB's Energy for All Initiative.[36] Cumulative investments in energy access was $9.02 billion for 2008 to 2018. All three indicators of energy access were higher than their respective baselines. First, the annual investment in energy access averaged $819.90 million in 2008 to 2018, which was almost six times the $140.45 million baseline. Second, the number of projects ranged from 5 to 20 annually in 2008 to 2018, which exceeded the baseline of 4 projects per year. Third, over 22 million households were given new or improved electricity connections from 2008 to 2018. The annual average was 2 million households, which was about 8 times over the baseline of 253,847 households.

Energy access improved as majority of the projects involved the improvement and expansion of the distribution systems, which amounted to about 67.9% of the total investment in energy access for 2008 to 2018. About 15.6% of the said total was invested in rural and off-grid electrification, and 14.4% in clean cooking and heating. Investments in heating focused on areas such as Pakistan and the PRC, while investments in cooking was relatively new.

Overall, the Clean Energy Program has been contributing to the Asia and Pacific region's efforts to have a low-carbon growth. For all the clean energy projects from 2008 to 2018, the cumulative carbon emission reduction was 144.25 million tons of carbon dioxide equivalent (tCO_2-eq). Its annual average was 13.11 tCO_2-eq, which is higher than the baseline of 8.2 million tCO_2-equivalent.

Employing clean energy—through renewable energy, energy efficiency, and energy access—will continue to be an integral part of the Asia and Pacific region's journey to sustainable low-carbon development. ADB would have to sustain and increase its efforts in assisting its developing member countries have access to clean modern energy, and together achieve the global commitments set in the SDGs and the Paris Agreement through the countries' Nationally Determined Contributions. With the help of the Clean Energy Program, ADB can help its developing member countries achieve Strategy 2030's goal of a prosperous, inclusive, resilient, and sustainable Asia and the Pacific.

---

[36] Counting of energy access projects has a methodology, which includes preparatory TA projects or facilitating energy access projects. Counting of clean energy investment projects follows a stricter methodology as it only counts climate mitigation projects.

APPENDIX 1

Clean Energy Projects (2008–2018)

Clean Energy Projects (2008)

DMC	Loan/ Grant No.	Project Name	ADB Investment	Clean Energy Investment
Sovereign Projects				
Energy Sector				
PRC	2408	Gansu Heihe Rural Hydropower Development Investment Program – Tranche 2: Dagushan Hydropower	28.00	28.00
IND	2415	National Power Grid Development Investment Program – Tranche 1	400.00	400.00
PRC	2426	Guangdong Energy Efficiency and Environment Improvement Investment Program – Tranche 1	35.00	35.00
VIE	2429	Song Bung 4 Hydropower	196.00	196.00
AZE	2437	Power Transmission Enhancement	160.00	11.20
PAK	2438	Power Distribution Enhancement Investment Program – Tranche 1	242.00	41.10
PAK	2439	Power Distribution Enhancement Investment Program – Tranche 1	10.00	1.70
IND	2461	Himachal Pradesh Clean Energy Development Investment Program – Tranche 1	150.00	150.00
BHU	2463	Green Power Development	51.00	51.00
BHU	2464	Green Power Development	29.00	29.00
IND	2498	Uttarakhand Power Sector Investment Program – Tranche 2	62.40	62.40
AFG	134	Energy Sector Development Investment Program – Tranche 1	164.00	22.10
AFG	9128	Development of Mini Hydroplants	12.00	12.00
BHU	141	Green Power Development	1.00	1.00
BHU	119	Green Power Development	25.28	25.28
MON	9127	Energy Conservation and Emission Reduction from Poor Households	2.00	2.00
Non-Energy Sector				
PRC	2407	Gansu Baiyin Urban Development	80.00	12.20
IND	2410	Uttarakhand Urban Sector Development Investment Program – Tranche 1	60.00	21.10
PRC	2420	Xinjiang Municipal Infrastructure and Environment Improvement	105.00	9.80
PAK	2424	Preparing the Lahore Rapid Mass Transit System	6.00	1.20
PRC	2428	Integrated Ecosystem and Water Resources Management in the Baiyangdan Basin	100.00	6.62
UZB	2466	Surkhandarya Water Supply and Sanitation	30.00	7.50
		Subtotal Sovereign Projects	**1,948.68**	**1,126.20**

continued on next page

Table continued

DMC	Loan/ Grant No.	Project Name	ADB Investment	Clean Energy Investment
	**Nonsovereign Projects**			
Energy Sector				
PHI	7273/2405	Masinloc Power Partners Company Limited (MPPC)	200.00	10.00
REG	7275	Asia Clean Energy Fund; China Clean Energy Capital; China Environment Fund III; GEF South Asia Clean Energy Fund; MAP Clean Energy Fund	100.00	100.00
IND	7276/2419	Coastal Gujarat Power Limited (CGPL)	450.00	90.00
IND	7277/2417	Gujarat Paguthan Energy Corp. Private Limited (GPEC) – Gujarat Paguthan Wind Energy Financing Facility	45.00	45.00
IND	7277/2434	CLP Wind Farms Private Limited (CWFPL)	60.00	60.00
PRC	7279/2422	Dalkia Asia Pte., Ltd. (Dalkia Asia) – Municipal District Energy Infrastructure Development	200.00	150.00
PRC	7279/2422	Dalkia Asia Pte., Ltd. (Dalkia Asia) – Municipal District Energy Infrastructure Development (B-Loan)	200.00	150.00
PRC	7285/2435	Datang Sino-Japan (Chifeng) Renewable Power Corporation – Inner Mongolia Wind Power	24.08	22.18
colspan=3	**Subtotal Nonsovereign Projects**	1,279.08	627.18
colspan=3	**GRAND TOTAL**	**3,227.76**	**1,753.38**

ADB = Asian Development Bank, AFG = Afghanistan, AZE = Azerbaijan, BHU = Bhutan, DMC = developing member country, IND = India, MON = Mongolia, PAK = Pakistan, PHI = Philippines, PRC = People's Republic of China, REG = regional, SRI = Sri Lanka, THA = Thailand, UZB = Uzbekistan, VIE = Viet Nam.
Source: ADB.

Clean Energy Projects (2009)

DMC	Loan/Grant No.	Project Name	ADB Investment	Clean Energy Investment
Sovereign Projects				
Energy Sector				
PRC	2611	MFF: Guangdong Energy Efficiency and Environment Improvement Investment Program-Tranche 2	22.06	22.06
IND	2510	National Power Grid Development Investment Program-Tranche 2	200.00	120.00
IND	2520	Madhya Pradesh Power Sector Investment Program-Tranche 5	166.00	47.70
IND	2596	Himachal Pradesh Clean energy Development Investment Program-Tranche 2	59.10	59.10
IND	2592	Assam Power Sector Enhancement Investment Program-Tranche 1	60.30	4.90
IND	2502	Uttarakhand Power Sector Investment Program-Tranche 3	30.60	30.60
NEP	2587	Energy Access and Efficiency Improvement Project	65.00	26.70
PAK	2552/3	Energy Efficiency Investment Program-Tranche 1	60.00	60.00
PHI	2507	Philippine Energy Efficiency Project	31.10	31.10
SRI	2518/9	Clean Energy and Access Improvement Project	160.00	32.90
VIE	2517	Renewable Energy Development Network Expansion and Rehabilitation for Remote Commune Sector	151.00	78.59
Non-Energy Sector				
CAM	2602	Rehabilitation of the Railway in Cambodia (Supplementary)	42.00	8.40
PRC	2574	Hebei Small Cities and Towns Development Demonstration Sector	100.00	3.14
PRC	2606	Shanxi Small Cities and Towns Development Demonstration Sector	100.00	8.70
PRC	2605	Railway Energy Efficiency and Safety Enhancement Investment Program (Tranche 1)	300.00	120.80
PRC	2601	Lanzhou Sustainable Urban Transport Project	150.00	27.35
IND	2506	Rajasthan Urban Sector Development Investment Program-Tranche 2	150.00	3.45
KGZ	2556	Issyk-Kul Sustainable Development Project	16.50	3.49
SRI	2557/8	Greater Colombo Wastewater Management Project	100.00	13.71
UZB	2564	Water Supply and Sanitation Services Investment Program-Tranche 1	60.00	21.20
VIE	2602	Quality and Safety Enhancement of Agricultural Products and Biogas Development Project	95.00	19.13
		Subtotal Sovereign Projects	**2,118.66**	**743.02**

continued on next page

Table continued

DMC	Loan/ Grant No.	Project Name	ADB Investment	Clean Energy Investment
Nonsovereign Projects				
Energy Sector				
PRC	7291/2505	Sanchuan Clean Energy Development Co. Ltd. (Small Hydropower Development Project)	203.57	203.57
PRC	7297/2512	Cecic Hke Wind Power Co. Ltd. (Zhangbie Wind Power Project)– A public sector, nonsovereign project	34.30	34.30
IND	7300	Public-Private Partnership for Renewable Energy development	40.00	40.00
REG	7304	Mekong Brahmaputra Clean Development Fund	15.00	15.00
THA	7290/2504	Biomass Co. (Biomass Power Project)	76.75	76.75
Non-Energy Sector				
PRC	7296	China Everbright Environmental Energy Limited-CEEEL (Municipal Waste-to-Energy Project)	200.00	200.00
		Subtotal Nonsovereign Projects	569.62	569.62
		GRAND TOTAL	2,688.28	1,312.64

ADB = Asian Development Bank, CAM = Cambodia, DMC = developing member country, IND = India, KGZ = Kyrgyz Republic, NEP = Nepal, PAK = Pakistan, PHI = Philippines, PRC = People's Republic of China, REG = regional, SRI = Sri Lanka, THA = Thailand, UZB = Uzbekistan, VIE = Viet Nam.

Source: ADB.

Clean Energy Projects (2010)

DMC	Loan/Grant No.	Project Name	ADB Investment	Clean Energy Investment
Sovereign Projects				
Energy Sector				
PRC	42117-013	Tianjin Integrated Gasification Combined Cycle Power Plant Project	135.00	36.45
INO	40061-013	Java-Bali Electricity Distribution Performance Improvement Project	50.00	39.95
BAN	38164-013	Natural Gas Access Improvement	266.00	154.18
UZB	43151-023	Talimarjan Power Project	350.00	120.02
AZE	43406-01	Janub Gas-Fired Power Plant Project	232.32	76.70
PRC	40634-013	Inner Mongolia Autonomous Region Environment Improvement Project (Phase II)	150.00	34.50
KGZ	43456-023	Power Sector Improvement Project	16.70	1.54
IND	41614-033	Assam Power Sector Enhancement Investment Program-Tranche 2	89.70	22.00
IND	41626-013	Bihar Power System Improvement Project	132.20	6.62
IND	41627-043	Himachal Pradesh Clean Energy Development Investment Program-Tranche 3	208.00	208.00
PNG	41504-023	Town Electrification Investment Program-Tranche 1	57.30	57.30
PAK	34339-033	MFF- Renewable Energy Development Sector Investment Program PFR2	200.00	200.00
PAK	38456-033	Power Distribution Enhancement Investment Program-Tranche 2	242.00	31.00
IND	32298-073	Madhya Pradesh Power Sector Investment Program - Tranche 6	69.00	26.80
PRC	196	Tianjin Integrated Gasification Combined Cycle Power Plant Project	5.00	1.35
INO	198	Java-Bali Electricity Distribution Performance Improvement Project	1.00	0.70
THA	201	Natural Energy Development Company (Solar Power Project)	2.00	2.00
KGZ	218	Power Sector Improvement Project	28.10	2.50
BHU	228	Rural Renewable Energy Development	21.59	21.59
RMI	9148	Improved Energy Supply For Poor Households	1.76	1.06
Non-Energy Sector				
PRC	2632	Integrated Renewable Biomass Energy Development Sector	66.10	66.10
UZB	2633	Water Supply and Sanitation Services Investment Program	140.00	1.64
NEP	2656	Kathmandu Sustainable Urban Transport	10.00	1.80
PAL	2691/2692	Water Sector improvement Program	16.00	0.89
BAN	2695	City Region Develoment Project	120.00	20.00
PRC	202	Integrated Renewable Biomass Energy Development Sector	3.00	3.00
INO	203	Integrated Renewable Biomass Energy Development Sector	9.20	9.20
THA	212	Kathmandu Sustainable Urban Transport	10.00	2.00
		Subtotal Sovereign Projects	**2,631.97**	**1,148.89**

continued on next page

Table continued

DMC	Loan/ Grant No.	Project Name	ADB Investment	Clean Energy Investment
Nonsovereign Projects				
Energy Sector				
AFG	7307	Sungas LLC (Sungas Liquefied Petroleum Gas Project)	8.00	2.76
THA	7311/2628	Natural Energy Development Company (Solar Power Project)	70.00	70.00
AZE	7313/637	Garadagh Cement Open Joint stock Company (Garadagh Cement Expansion and Energy Efficiency Improvement Project)	27.00	0.32
THA	7314/ 676	Bangchak Petroleum Public Company (BCP)-Bangchak Solar Power Project	134.31	134.31
PRC	7316/2693	Zhongran Investment Limited (ZIL)-Municipal Gas Infrastructure Development Project (Phase 2)	200.00	83.24
PRC	7317/2698	Tianjin Xiehe Wind Power Investment Company Limited (TXWP)(Jilin Wind Power Project)	240.00	240.00
PAK	7319/2704	Zorlu Enerji Power Project	36.80	36.80
REG	7320/21	Proposed Equity Investments Clean Resources Asia Growth Fund and Renewable Energy Asia Fund	40.00	40.00
		Subtotal Nonsovereign Projects	756.11	607.43
		GRAND TOTAL	3,388.08	1,756.32

ADB = Asian Development Bank, AFG = Afghanistan, AZE = Azerbaijan, BAN = Bangladesh, BHU = Bhutan, CAM = Cambodia, DMC = developing member country, IND = India, INO = Indonesia, KGZ = Kyrgyz Republic, NEP = Nepal, PAK = Pakistan, PAL = Palau, PRC = People's Republic of China, REG = regional, RMI = Republic of the Marshall Islands.
Source: ADB.

Clean Energy Projects (2011)

DMC	Loan/ Grant No.	Project Name	ADB Investment	Clean Energy Investment
		Sovereign Projects		
Energy Sector				
BAN	2769	Power System Efficiency Improvement Project	300.00	101.86
PRC	2771	Shandong Energy Efficiency and Emission reduction Project	100.00	100.00
PRC	2773	Guangdong Energy Efficiency and Environment Improvement Investment Program-Tranche 3	42.94	42.94
PRC	2835	Hebei Energy Efficiency Improvement and Emission Reduction Project	100.00	100.00
IND	2764	Madhya Pradesh Energy Efficiency Improvement Investment Program-Tranche 1	200.00	51.85
IND	2830	Madhya Pradesh Energy Efficiency Improvement Investment Program-Tranche 2	200.00	51.85
IND	2800	Assam Power Sector Enhancement Investment Program-Tranche 3	50.00	3.51
IND	2778	Gujarat Solar Power Transmission Project	100.00	100.00
IND	2794	Himachal Pradesh Clean Energy Transmission investment Program-Tranche 1	113.00	113.00
IND	2787	National Grid Improvement Project	500.00	15.45
LAO	2818/2819	GMS Nam Ngum 3 Hydropower Project	115.12	115.12
NEP	2808	Electricity Transmission Expansion and Supply Improvement Project	56.00	2.30
SRI	2733/2734	Sustainable Power Sector Support Project	120.00	11.73
UZB	2779	Advanced electricity Metering Project	150.00	28.13
VIE	2814	O Mon IV combined Cycle Power Plant Project	309.89	76.40
AFG	0280/1/2	Energy Sector Development Investment Program-Tranche 3 (Gereshk Electricity Services Improvement project)	75.40	27.42
BAN	0253/0254	Public-private Infrastructure Development Facility	3.30	3.30
Non-Energy Sector				
PRC	2738	Qinghai Rural Water Resources Management	60.00	45.32
PRC	2759	Xinjiang Altay Urban Infrastructure & Environment Improvement Project	100.00	4.75
PRC	2760	Gansu Tianshui Urban Infrastructure Development Project	100.00	12.25
PRC	2765	Railway Energy Efficiency and Safety Enhancement Investment Program-Tranche 3	250.00	50.00
IND	2793	Railway Sector Investment Program-Tranche 1	150.00	27.27
TKM	2737	North-South Railway project	125.00	25.00
VIE	2741	Ha Noi Metro Rail System Project-Line 3	293.00	58.60
VIE	2754	Water Sector Investment Program-Tranche 1	138.00	32.00
		Subtotal Sovereign Projects	**3,751.65**	**1,200.05**

continued on next page

Table continued

DMC	Loan/ Grant No.	Project Name	ADB Investment	Clean Energy Investment
Nonsovereign Projects				
Energy Sector				
BAN	45916/7349/2844	Industrial Energy Efficiency Program (Industrial Infrastructure Development Finance company)	30.00	30.00
IND	7331	Solar Power Generation	150.00	150.00
IND	7338/2788	National Grid Improvement project (formerly Power Grid)	250.00	7.72
IND	7340/2798	Dahanu Solar Power Private Limited	48.00	48.00
LAO	7341/2799	Nam Ngum 3 Power Company	350.00	350.00
PAK	7339/2792	Star Hydro Power Limited (Patrind Hydropower Project)	97.00	97.00
PAK	49505-01/7348	Foundation Wind Energy Project I	33.43	33.43
PAK	49505-02/7348	Foundation Wind Energy Project II	33.18	33.18
THA	7335/2762	Gulf JP NS Company Limited (Nong Saeng Natural Gas Power Project)	170.00	38.58
Non-Energy Sector				
PRC	7336	Sino-Green Climate Investment Fund	25.00	25.00
IND	7329/2748	Bangalore Metro Rail System Project	250.00	50.00
INO	7327/2740	Indonesia Exim Bank	200.00	30.00
REG	7332/7333/7334	Equity Investment in Climatech Venture Capital Funds	40.00	40.00
		Subtotal Nonsovereign Projects	**1,676.61**	**932.91**
		GRAND TOTAL	**5,428.26**	**2,132.96**

ADB = Asian Development Bank, AFG = Afghanistan, BAN = Bangladesh, DMC = developing member country, IND = India, INO = Indonesia, LAO = Lao People's Democratic Republic, NEP = Nepal, PAK = Pakistan, PRC = People's Republic of China, REG = regional, SRI = Sri Lanka, TKM = Turkmenistan, UZB = Uzbekistan, VIE = Viet Nam.
Source: ADB.

Clean Energy Projects (2012)

DMC	Loan/ Grant No.	Project Name	ADB Investment	Clean Energy Investment
Sovereign Projects				
Energy Sector				
KGZ	2869	Power Sector Rehabilitation Project	15.00	12.10
PRC	2885	Shanxi Energy Efficiency and Environment Improvement Project	100.00	41.13
PRC	2898	Heilongjiang Energy Efficient District Heating Project	150.00	61.70
PHI	2964	Market Transformation Through Introduction of Energy-Efficient Electric Vehicle Project	400.00	304.57
SRI	2892	Clean Energy and Network Improvement Project	100.00	5.13
SRI	2893	Clean Energy and Network Improvement Project	30.00	1.54
IND	2914	Himachal Pradesh Clean Energy Development Investment Program-Tranche 4	315.00	315.00
IND	2924	Uttarakhand Power Sector Investment Program-Project 4	150.00	150.00
BAN	2966	Power System Expansion and Efficiency Improvement Investment Program-Tranche 1	185.00	35.65
KGZ	294	Power Sector Rehabilitation Project	40.00	27.90
PHI	326	Market Transformation Through Introduction of Energy-Efficient Electric Vehicle Project	5.00	5.00
SRI	303	Clean Energy and Network Improvement Project	1.50	1.50
Non-Energy Sector				
VIE	2968	Low-Carbon Agricultural Support Project	74.00	74.00
BAN	2864	Greater Dhaka Sustainable Urban Transport Project	100.00	12.59
BAN	2862/3	Greater Dhaka Sustainable Urban Transport Project	60.00	7.55
MON	2934	MFF: Urban Transport Development Investment Program-Tranche 1	29.70	2.10
MON	2935	MFF: Urban Transport Development Investment Program-Tranche 1	30.20	2.14
VIE	2956	Ho Chi Minh City Urban Mass Rapid Transit Line 2 Investment Program-Tranche 2	500.00	100.00
PRC	2962	Hunan Xiangjiang Inland Waterway Transport Project (Hydropower Component)	150.00	150.00
BAN	2865	Financing Brick Kiln Efficiency Improvement Project	30.00	30.00
BAN	2866	Financing Brick Kiln Efficiency Improvement Project	20.00	20.00
ARM	2860	Water Supply and Sanitation Sector Project (additional financing)	40.00	2.56
		Subtotal Sovereign Projects	**2,525.40**	**1,362.16**

continued on next page

Table continued

DMC	Loan/ Grant No.	Project Name	ADB Investment	Clean Energy Investment
Nonsovereign Projects				
Energy Sector				
IND	7353/2853	ICICI Renewable Energy and Energy Efficiency Projects	100.00	100.00
IND	7354/2854	Rajasthan Concentrating Solar Power Project (Rajasthan Sun Technique Energy Private Limited)	103.00	103.00
THA	7356/2875	Bangchak Solar Energy Company Limited (Provincial solar Power Project)	37.80	37.80
THA	7370/2912	Gulf JP UT Company Limited (Ayudhaya Natural Gas Project)	185.00	107.29
THA	7376/2945	Theppana Wind Farm Company Limited (Theppana Wind Power Project)	8.20	8.17
PRC	7368/2899	China Everbright Biomass Energy Investment Limited (Agricultural Waste-to-Energy Project)	120.00	120.00
PRC	7368/2900	China Everbright Environmental Energy Limited (Municipal Waste-to-Energy Project)	80.00	80.00
IND	7361/2906 to 7366/2911	145-MW Grid-connected Solar Project (5 loan projects combined)	100.00	100.00
REG	7371/2919	Southeast Asia Energy Efficiency Project	40.00	40.00
Non-Energy Sector				
REG	7352	Climate Public-Private Partnership Fund (Customized Fund Investment Group)	100.00	100.00
PRC	7377/2919	Dynagreen Environmental Protection Group Company (Dynagreen Waste-to-Energy Project)	200.00	200.00
		Subtotal Nonsovereign Projects	**1,074.00**	**996.26**
		GRAND TOTAL	**3,599.40**	**2,358.42**

ADB = Asian Development Bank, ARM = Armenia, BAN = Bangladesh, DMC = developing member country, IND = India, KGZ = Kyrgyz Republic, MON = Mongolia, PHI = Philippines, PRC = People's Republic of China, SRI = Sri Lanka, REG = regional, THA = Thailand, UZB = Uzbekistan, VIE = Viet Nam.
Source: ADB.

Clean Energy Projects (2013)

DMC	Loan/ Grant No.	Project Name	ADB Investment	Clean Energy Investment
Sovereign Projects				
Energy Sector				
BAN	3046	Second Public–Private Infrastructure Development Facility	10.00	10.00
BHU	3024	Green Power Development Project-Additional Financing	39.00	39.00
FSM	3004/3005	Yap Renewable Energy Development	9.04	6.35
IND	3001	Himachal Pradesh Clean Energy Transmission Investment Program-Tranche 2	110.00	110.00
IND	3052/8275	Rajasthan Renewable Energy Transmission Investment Program-Tranche 1	150.00	150.00
IND	3066	Madhya Pradesh Power Transmission and Distribution System Improvement Project	350.00	93.06
INO	3015	West Kalimantan Power Grid Strengthening Project	99.00	99.00
MYA	3084	Power Distribution Improvement Project	60.00	60.00
NEP	2990/2991	Tanahu Hydropower Project	150.00	150.00
PAK	3090/3091/92	Jamshoro Power Generation	900.00	109.07
PNG	2998/2999	Port Moresby Power Grid Development Project	66.70	29.40
PRC	3075	Qinghai Delingha Conscentrated Solar Power Thermal Project	150.00	150.00
UZB	3058/3059	Samarkand Solar Power Project	110.00	110.00
CAM	336	Rural Energy Project	6.11	0.22
IND	8275	Rajasthan Renewable Energy Transmission Investment Program	2.00	2.00
INO	354	West Kalimantan Power Grid Strengthening Project	2.00	2.00
NEP	361	Project Preparatory Facility for Energy	21.00	21.00
NEP	2990/2991	Tanahu Hydropower Project TA Grant	1.50	1.50
PRC	364	Hebei Energy Efficiency Improvement and Emission Reduction-Additional Financing to Loan 2835	3.65	3.65
SAM	370/373	Renewable Energy Development & Power Sector Rehabilitation Project	19.21	19.21
TAJ	376	Golovnaya 240-MW Hydropower Plant Rehabilitation Project	136.00	136.00
TON	347	Outer Island Renewable Energy Project	6.50	6.50
Non-Energy Sector				
BAN	3051	Dhaka Environmentally Sustainable Water Supply Project	250.00	49.33
BAN	3097	Railway Sector Investment Program-Tranche 3	100.00	20.00
IND	3048	Accelerating Infrastructure Investment Facility-Tranche 1	400.00	24.73
IND	3062	Jaipur Metro Rail Line 1- Phase B Project	176.00	35.20

continued on next page

Table continued

DMC	Loan/ Grant No.	Project Name	ADB Investment	Clean Energy Investment
IND	3053	Kolkata Environmental Improvement Investment Program - Tranche 1	100.00	10.42
LAO	3041	Water Supply and Sanitation Sector Project	35.00	15.94
PRC	3014	Hubei-Yichang Sustainable Urban Transport Project	150.00	6.30
PRC	3082	Railway Energy Efficiency and Safety Enhancement Investment Program-Tranche 4	180.00	36.00
SRI	3029/3030	Greater Colombo Water and Wastewater Management Improvement Investment Program-Tranche 2	88.00	8.62
UZB	3025	Amu Bukhara Irrigation System Rehabilitation Project	220.00	170.23
PRC	7392	Beijing Enterprises Water Group Limited and BEWG Environmental Group Company Limited (Wastewater Treatment and Reuse Project)	0.50	0.50
VIE	365	Energy Efficiency for Ho Chi Minh City Water Supply	2.00	2.00
		Subtotal Sovereign Projects	**4,103.21**	**1,687.23**
		Nonsovereign Projects		
Energy Sector				
ARM	7385	International Energy Corporation (Sevan-Hrazdan Cascade Hydropower System Rehabilitation Project)	25.00	25.00
IND	7396/3085	Petronet LNG Limited	150.00	16.17
IND	7398/3101	BSES Rajdhani Power Limited (Delhi Electricity Distribution Improvement Project)	80.00	12.80
IND	7386	NSL Renewable Power Private Limited (Hydro and Wind Power Development Project)	30.00	30.00
IND	7381	SIMPA Networks Off-grid Pay-as-you-go Solar Power Project	2.00	2.00
IND	7400	Welspun Renewables Energy Limited (WREL)-Solar and Wind Power Development	50.00	50.00
INO	7397/3089	Sarulla Geothermal Power Development Project	350.00	350.00
THA	7384/2992	Solarco company Limited (Central Thailand Solar Power Project)	87.00	87.00
Non-Energy Sector				
PRC	7380/2986	Clean Bus Leasing in PRC	275.00	66.80
PRC	7392	Beijing Enterprises Water Group Limited and BEWG Environmental Group Company Limited (Wastewater Treatment and Reuse Project)	240.00	29.72
		Subtotal Nonsovereign Projects	**1,289.00**	**669.49**
		GRAND TOTAL	**5,392.21**	**2,356.72**

ARM = Armenia, BAN = Bangladesh, BHU = Bhutan, CAM = Cambodia, DMC = developing member country, FSM = Federated States of Micronesia, IND = India, INO = Indonesia, LAO = Lao People's Democratic Republic, MYA = Myanmar, NEP = Nepal, PAK = Pakistan, PNG = Papua New Guinea, PRC = People's Republic of China, SAM = Samoa, SRI = Sri Lanka, TAJ = Tajikistan, TON = Tonga, UZB = Uzbekistan, VIE = Viet Nam.
Source: ADB.

Clean Energy Projects (2014)

DMC	Loan/Grant No.	Project Name	ADB Investment	Clean Energy Investment
	**Sovereign Projects**			
Energy Sector				
BHU	3225/3226	Second Green Power Development Project	95.25	86.67
COO	3193	Renewable Energy Sector Project	11.19	11.19
IND	3140	Assam Power Sector Investment Program-Tranche 1	50.00	32.27
IND	3186	Clean Energy Finance Investment Program-Tranche 1	200.00	200.00
KGZ	3212	Toktogul Rehabilitation Phase 2 Project	165.50	163.74
NEP	3139	South Asia Subregional Economic Cooperation Power System Expansion Project	180.00	5.00
PRC	3218	Low-Carbon District Heating Supply in Hohhot in Inner Mongolia Autonomous Region	150.00	64.27
SOL	3127	Provincial Renewable Energy Project	6.00	6.00
SRI	3146/3147	Green Power Development and Energy Efficiency Improvement Investment Program-Tranche 1	180.00	180.00
UZB	3141	Takhiatash Power Plant Efficiency Improvement Project	300.00	163.27
VIE	3161/8286	Hanoi and Ho Chi Minh City Power Grid Development	272.70	159.73
BHU	421	Second Green Power Development Project	25.25	25.25
COO	415	Renewable Energy Sector Project	7.26	7.26
KGZ	419	Toktogul Rehabilitation Phase 2 Project	44.50	37.36
MLD	409/410	Preparing Outer Islands for Sustainable Energy Development Project	50.00	50.00
NAU	414/424	Electricity Supply Security and Sustainability	4.70	0.80
NEP	398	South Asia Subregional Economic Cooperation Power System Expansion Project	11.20	10.00
SOL	386	Provincial Renewable Energy Project	6.00	6.00
VIE	384	Renewable Energy Development and Network Expansion and Rehabilitation for Remote Communes Sector-Additional Financing	3.00	3.00
Non-Energy Sector				
BAN	3169/3170	South Asia Subregional Economic Cooperation Railway Connectivity: Akhaura-Laksam Double Track	505.00	287.28
IND	3183	Rajasthan Urban Sector Development Program	250.00	30.77
PRC	3109	Railway Energy Efficiency and Safety Enhancement Investment Program-Tranche 5	170.00	59.70
PRC	3114	Guangdong Chaonan Water Resources Development and Protection Demonstration Project	100.00	9.98
PRC	3211	Jilin Urban Development	150.00	8.83
PRC	3216	Jiangxi Fuzhou Urban Integrated Infrastructure Improvement – Additional Financing	120.00	2.71

continued on next page

Table continued

DMC	Loan/ Grant No.	Project Name	ADB Investment	Clean Energy Investment
VIE	3113/8279	Sustainable Urban Transport for Ho Chi Minh City Mass Rapid Transit Line 2 Project	58.95	29.02
VIE	3235/8291	Strengthening Sustainable Urban Transport for Ha Noi Metro Line 3	53.15	26.17
NEP	383	South Asia Tourism Infrastructure Development Project–Additional Financing	3.00	3.00
PRC	420/388	Jiangxi Ji'an Sustainable Urban Transport Project	5.10	5.10
		Subtotal Sovereign Projects	**3,177.75**	**1,674.37**
		Nonsovereign Projects		
Energy Sector				
BAN	7436/3236	Summit Bibiyana II Power Company Limited (Bibiyana II Gas Power Project)	75.00	22.83
GEO	7407/3130	Adjaristsqali Hydropower Project	90.00	90.00
IND	7406	ReNew Power Ventures Private Limited (ReNew Power Investment Project)	50.00	50.00
IND	7416/3175	ACME Gurgaon Power Private Ltd.	9.79	9.79
IND	7417/3176	ACME Mumbai Power Private Ltd.	9.81	9.81
IND	7418/3177	ACME Rajdhani Power Private Ltd.	9.79	9.79
IND	7419/3178	ACME Medha Power Private Ltd.	9.81	9.81
IND	7420/3179	ACME Ranji Power Private Ltd.	10.79	10.79
IND	7421/3180	ACME-EDF Solar Power Project	50.00	50.00
INO	7409	Rantau Dedap Geothermal Development Project (Phase 1)	50.00	50.00
LAO	7417/3153	Nam Ngiep 1 Power Company Limited (Nam Ngiep 1 Hydropower Project)	127.00	127.00
LAO	7417/3154	Nam Ngiep 1 Power Company Limited (Nam Ngiep 1 Hydropower Project)	94.00	94.00
PRC	7432/3206	China Gas Holdings Limited (Natural Gas for Land and River Transportation Project)	450.00	109.35
REG	7430	Equity Investment in AEP II	30.00	30.00
THA	7435/3219	Chaiyaphum Wind Farm Company Limited (Subyai Wind Power Project)	83.00	83.00
Non-Energy Sector				
MYA	7408/3137	Yangon Urban Renewal and District Cooling Project	120.00	3.00
		Subtotal Nonsovereign Projects	**1,268.99**	**759.17**
		GRAND TOTAL	**4,446.74**	**2,433.52**

ADB = Asian Development Bank, BAN = Bangladesh, BHU = Bhutan, COO = Cook Islands, DMC = developing member country, GEO = Georgia, IND = India, INO = Indonesia, KGZ = Kyrgyz Republic, LAO = Lao People's Democratic Republic, MLD = Maldives, MYA = Myanmar, NAU = Nauru, NEP = Nepal, PRC = People's Republic of China, REG = regional, SOL = Solomon Islands, THA = Thailand, VIE = Viet Nam.
Source: ADB.

Clean Energy Projects (2015)

DMC	Loan/Grant No.	Project Name	ADB Investment	Clean Energy Investment
Sovereign Projects				
Energy Sector				
BAN	3350	Power System Expansion and Efficiency Improvement Investment Program-Tranche 3	205.00	50.00
IND	3327	Assam Power Sector Investment Program-Tranche 2	48.00	18.00
IND	3365	Green Energy Corridor and Grid Strengthening Project	500.00	141.50
IND	3365	Green Energy Corridor and Grid Strengthening Project		13.83
INO	3303	Sustainable and Inclusive Energy Program (Subprogram 1)	400.00	233.32
INO	3303	Sustainable and Inclusive Energy Program (Subprogram 1)	100.00	58.33
INO	3339	Electricity Grid Strengthening-Sumatra Program	575.00	172.50
INO	3339	Electricity Grid Strengthening-Sumatra Program	25.00	7.50
PAK	3328	Second Power Distribution Enhancement Investment Program-Tranche 1	380.00	97.31
PAK	3329	Second Power Distribution Enhancement Investment Program-Tranche 1	20.00	5.12
PAK	3321	Sustainable Energy Sector Reform Program (Subprogram 2)	100.00	10.00
PAK	3322	Sustainable Energy Sector Reform Program (Subprogram 2)	300.00	30.00
PRC	3308	Chemical Industry Energy Efficiency and Emission Reduction Project	100.00	95.00
PRC	3356	Beijing-Tianjin-Hebei Air Quality Improvement-Hebei Policy Reform Program	300.00	117.70
PRC	3358	Qingdao Smart Low-Carbon District Energy Project	130.00	89.83
UZB	3286	Advanced Electricity Metering Phase 4 Project	300.00	44.11
UZB	3285	Northwest Region Power Transmission Line	150.00	17.05
CAM	468	Medium Voltage Sub-Transmission Expansion Sector-Additional Financing	1.00	1.00
CAM	336	Rural Energy Project	0.36	0.36
MLD	429	Preparing Outer Island for Sustainable Development-Additional Financing	5.00	5.00
TON	444	Outer Island Renewable Energy Project-Additional Financing	1.44	0.05
TON	445	Outer Island Renewable Energy Project-Additional Financing	3.57	0.12
TON	446	Outer Island Renewable Energy Project-Additional Financing	0.75	0.03
SAM	456	Renewable Energy Development and Power Sector Rehabilitation- Additional Financing	5.06	5.06
SAM	457	Renewable Energy Development and Power Sector Rehabilitation- Additional Financing	2.49	2.49

continued on next page

Table continued

DMC	Loan/ Grant No.	Project Name	ADB Investment	Clean Energy Investment
Non-Energy Sector				
BAN	3301	Railway Rolling Stock Project	200.00	200.00
IND	3337	North Eastern Region Capital Cities Development Investment Program – Tranche 3	80.00	21.92
IND	3307	Accelerating Infrastructure Investment Facility in India – Tranche 2	300.00	159.00
LAO	3250	Vientiane Sustainable Urban Transport Project	50.00	50.00
MYA	3316	Mandalay Urban Services Improvement Project	60.00	2.00
PRC	3277	Hubei Enshi Qing River Upstream Environment Rehabilitation Project	100.00	2.03
PRC	3262	Xinjiang Akesu Integrated Urban Development Improvement Project	150.00	25.90
PRC	3263	Xinjiang Tacheng Border Cities and Counties Development Improvement Project	150.00	30.49
PRC	3296	Henan Sustainable Livestock Farming and Product Safety Demonstration Project	69.00	10.00
VIE	3363	Ha Noi Metro Line System Project (Line 3: Nhon-Ha Noi Station Section) (Additional Financing)	59.00	59.00
VIE	3364	Ha Noi Metro Line System Project (Line 3: Nhon-Ha Noi Station Section) (Additional Financing)	5.80	5.80
VIE	8302	Ha Noi Metro Line System Project (Line 3: Nhon-Ha Noi Station Section) (Additional Financing)	50.00	50.00
LAO	471	Vientiane Sustainable Urban Transport Project	1.84	1.84
		Subtotal Sovereign Projects	**4,928.31**	**1,833.19**
		Nonsovereign Projects		
Energy Sector				
IND	8298	Simpa Energy Private Limited (Off-Grid Prepaid Solar Leasing Project)	6.00	6.00
IND	7467/3375	Green Energy Corridor and Grid Strengthening Project	500.00	141.50
IND	7467/3375	Green Energy Corridor and Grid Strengthening Project		13.83
PAK	7445/3252	Mira Power Limited (Gulpur Hydropower Project)	65.00	65.00
PHI	7442/3246	EDC Burgos Wind Power Corporation (150-MW Burgos Wind Farm Project)	20.00	20.00
THA	7362/3366	Northeastern Thailand Wind Power Project-Banchuan Development	31.50	31.50
THA	7363/3367	Northeastern Thailand Wind Power Project-Benjarat Development	31.50	31.50
THA	7364/3368	Northeastern Thailand Wind Power Project-Nayangklak Development	31.50	31.50

continued on next page

Table continued

DMC	Loan/ Grant No.	Project Name	ADB Investment	Clean Energy Investment
THA	7365/3369	Northeastern Thailand Wind Power Project-Nayangklak Wind Power	31.50	31.50
THA	7366/3370	Northeastern Thailand Wind Power Project-Pongnok Development	31.50	31.50
THA	8301	Northeastern Thailand Wind Power Project	18.90	18.90
Non-Energy Sector				
PHI	7551/3266	AP Renewables Inc. (Tiwi and Makban Geothermal Power Green Bonds Project)	181.17	181.17
PHI	7551/3266	AP Renewables Inc. (Tiwi and Makban Geothermal Power Green Bonds Project)	40.64	40.64
		Subtotal Nonsovereign Projects	**989.21**	**644.54**
		GRAND TOTAL	**5,917.52**	**2,477.73**

ADB = Asian Development Bank, BAN = Bangladesh, CAM = Cambodia, DMC = developing member country , IND = India, INO = Indonesia, KGZ = Kyrgyz Republic, LAO = Lao People's Democratic Republic, MLD = Maldives, MYA = Myanmar, NAU = Nauru, NEP = Nepal, PAK = Pakistan, PHI = Philippines, PRC = People's Republic of China, REG = regional, SAM = Samoa, THA = Thailand, TON = Tonga, UZB = Uzbekistan, VIE = Viet Nam.
Source: ADB.

Clean Energy Projects (2016)

DMC	Loan/ Grant No.	Project Name	ADB Investment	Clean Energy Investment
Sovereign Projects				
Energy Sector				
AZE	3407	Power Distribution Enhancement Investment Program-Tranche 1	250.00	168.00
SRI	3409	Supporting Electricity Supply Reliability Improvement	115.00	25.00
KGZ	3422	Toktogul Rehabilitation Phase 3	100.00	88.37
PAK	3419/3420	Second Power Transmission Enhancement Investment Program-Tranche 1	125.00	5.00
IND	3436	Demand-Side Energy Efficiency Investment Project	200.00	200.00
PRC	3504	Air Quality Improvement in Greater Beijing, Tianjin, Hebei Region (China National Investment and Guaranty Corporation's Green Financing Platform Project)	499.60	340.00
SRI	3483/3484/8313	Green Power Development and Energy Efficiency Improvement Investment Program-Tranche 2	180.00	36.00
IND	3282/8312	Rajasthan Renewable Energy Transmission Program - Tranche 2	348.00	346.00
PRC	3475	Shaanxi Accelerated Energy Efficiency and Environment Improvement Financing Program	150.00	150.00
PAK	3476	Access to Clean Energy Investment Project	325.00	247.00
COO	493	Renewable Energy Sector-Additional Financing	4.27	4.27
KGZ	494	Toktogul Rehabilitation Phase 3	50.00	44.18
SOL	514	Solar Power Development Project	2.24	2.24
SOL	515	Solar Power Development Project	6.20	6.20
NEP	520	South Asia Subregional Economic Cooperation Power System Expansion-Additional financing	20.00	20.00
SRI	486	Supporting Electricity Supply Reliability Improvement	1.80	1.80
Subtotal Sovereign Projects			**2,377.11**	**1,684.06**
Nonsovereign Projects				
Energy Sector				
IND	7474/3381	Mytrah Vayu (Ravalpalli) Pvt. Limited	18.00	18.00
IND	7475/3382	Mytrah Vayu (Savalsang II) Pvt. Limited	23.00	23.00
IND	7476/3383	Mytrah Aadhya Power Pvt. Limited	14.00	14.00
IND	7477/3384	Mytrah Aakash Power Pvt. Limited	14.00	14.00
IND	7478/3385	Mytrah Vayu (Som) Pvt. Limited	42.00	42.00
IND	7479/3386	Mytrah Vayu (Tungabhadra) Pvt. Limited	64.00	64.00
THA	7483/3412	Stumpf Energy Solutions (Thailand) and Stumpf Energy Tranche B (Distributed Commercial Solar Power)	47.00	47.00
REG	7485	Fluidic (Distributed Energy Storage Solution)	5.00	5.00
PAK	7487/3448	Triconboston Consulting Corporation (Private) Limited (Triconboston Wind power)	75.00	75.00

continued on next page

Table continued

DMC	Loan/ Grant No.	Project Name	ADB Investment	Clean Energy Investment
CAM	7498/3495/ 8317	Sunseap Asset (Cambodia) Co. Ltd. (Cambodia Solar Power)	9.85	9.85
IND	7495/3448	ReNew Private Ventures Private Limited (ReNew Clean Energy Project)	389.20	389.20
INO	7495/3448	PT. Supreme Muara Laboh (Muara Laboh Geothermal Power Project)	109.25	109.25
THA	7494/3490	Thai-Sunseap Asset Company Limited (Grid Parity Rooftop Solar Project)	43.56	43.56
		Subtotal Nonsovereign Projects	**853.86**	**853.86**
		GRAND TOTAL	**3,230.97**	**2,537.92**

ADB = Asian Development Bank, AZE = Azerbaijan, CAM = Cambodia, COO = Cook Islands, DMC = developing member country, IND = India, KGZ = Kyrgyz Republic, NEP = Nepal, PAK = Pakistan, PRC = People's Republic of China, REG = regional, SRI = Sri Lanka, SOL = Solomon Islands, THA = Thailand.

Source: ADB.

Clean Energy Projects (2017)

DMC	Loan/ Grant No.	Project Name	ADB Investment	Clean Energy Investment
	Sovereign Projects			
Energy Sector				
PAK	3537	Sustainable Energy Sector Reform Program – Subprogram 3	300.00	20.00
PRC	3629	Air Quality Improvement in the Greater Beijing-Tianjin-Hebei Region-China Energy Conservation and Environment Protection Group's Emission Control and Pollution Reduction Fund	1,500.00	199.00
PNG	3544/3545	Town Electrification Investment Program – Tranche 2	60.90	60.90
PNG	3545	Town Electrification Investment Program – Tranche 2	5.00	
VAN	3572	Energy Access Project	2.50	2.50
BAN	3522/3523	Bangladesh Power System Enhancement and Efficiency Improvement Project	616.00	11.20
IND	3521	Solar Transmission Sector Project	175.00	175.00
NEP	3542	Power Transmission and Distribution Efficiency Enhancement Project	150.00	150.00
SRI	3571	Solar Rooftop Power Generation Project	50.00	25.00
SRI	3585	Wind Power Generation Project	200.00	198.00
INO	3561	Sustainable and Inclusive Energy Subprogram 2	400.00	230.00
INO	3560	Sustainable Energy Access in Eastern Indonesia-Electricity Grid Development Program	600.00	72.35
AFG	545	MFF Energy Supply Improvement Investment Program (Solar), Tranche 3	44.76	43.96
VAN	543	Energy Access Project	2.50	2.50
RMI	554	Majuro Power Network Strengthening Project (Majuro Electricity System Strengthening Project)	2.00	1.14
		Subtotal Sovereign Projects	**4,108.66**	**1,191.55**
	Nonsovereign Projects			
Energy Sector				
ARM	3540	Electric Networks of Armenia (ENA) Distribution Network	80.00	80.00
IND	3622	Ostro Kutch Wind Private Limited (Kutch Wind Project)	100.00	100.00
PAK	7530/3596	Zorlu Solar Pakistan (Private) Limited (Zorlu Solar Power)	20.00	20.00
PRC	3637/3638	Arctic Green Energy and Sinopec Green Energy Geothermal Development (Geothermal District Heating)	250.00	250.00
PRC	7512	China Everbright Greentech Ltd. (China Everbright Renewable Energy Project)	10.00	10.00
VIE	7534/3607	China Everbright International Limited (Municipal Waste-to-Energy Project)	100.00	100.00
INO	7533/3606	PT Energi Bayu Jeneponto (Eastern Indonesia Renewable Energy – Phase 1)	56.35	56.35
REG	7513	B. Grimm Power Public Company Ltd (ASEAN Distributed Power Project-Phase 1)	75.00	75.00

continued on next page

Table continued

DMC	Loan/ Grant No.	Project Name	ADB Investment	Clean Energy Investment
REG	7523/3578	B. Grimm Power Public Company Limited (ASEAN Distributed Power Project-Phase 2)	235.00	117.50
SAM	7515/3553	Jarcon PTY Limited and Sun Pacific Energy Limited (Solar Power Development-Samoa)	2.00	2.00
THA	7524/3581	Chana Green Company Limited (Southern Thailand Waste-to Energy Project)	33.60	33.60
		Subtotal Nonsovereign Projects	**961.95**	**844.45**
		GRAND TOTAL	**5,070.61**	**2,036.00**

ADB = Asian Development Bank, AFG = Afghanistan, ARM = Armenia, BAN = Bangladesh, DMC = developing member country, IND = India, INO = Indonesia, NEP = Nepal, PAK = Pakistan, PNG = Papua New Guinea, PRC = People's Republic of China, REG = regional, RMI = Republic of the Marshall Islands, SAM = Samoa, SRI = Sri Lanka, THA = Thailand, TON = Tonga, UZB = Uzbekistan, VAN = Vanuatu, VIE = Viet Nam.

Source: ADB.

Clean Energy Projects (2018)

DMC	Loan/Grant Number	Project Name	ADB Investment	Clean Energy Investment
Sovereign Projects				
Energy Sector				
PAK	3677	MFF Power Transmission Enhancement Investment Program II Tranche 3	280.00	52.00
TKM	3734	National Power Grid Strengthening Project	500.00	3.40
MON	3708	Upscaling Renewable Energy Sector Project	40.00	40.00
PRC	3765	Air Quality Improvement in the Greater Beijing-Tianjin-Hebei-Shandong Clean Heating and Cooling Project	399.91	360.00
BAN	3683	Southwest Transmission Grid Expansion Project	350.00	86.00
BAN	3676	Rupsha 800-MW Combined Cycle Power Plant Project	500.00	14.28
IND	3733	Himachal Pradesh Clean Energy Transmission Investment Program - Tranche 3	105.00	100.63
NEP	3721	South Asia Subregional Economic Cooperation Power System Expansion Project-Additional Financing	20.00	20.00
MYA	3748	Power Network Development Project	298.90	101.00
AFG	634	Energy Supply Improvement Investment Program-Tranche 5	143.42	97.00
TAJ	622	Reconnection to Central Asian Power System Project	35.00	35.00
TON	586	Outer Islands Renewable Energy Project-Additional Financing	5.50	2.43
Subtotal Sovereign Projects			**2,677.73**	**911.74**
Nonsovereign Projects				
INO	3647	Rantau Dedap Geothermal Power Project (Phase 2)	177.50	177.50
INO	7550/3653	Eastern Indonesia Renewable Energy Project (Phase 2)	5.97	5.97
INO	7551/3654	Eastern Indonesia Renewable Energy Project (Phase 2)	2.20	2.20
INO	7552/3655	Eastern Indonesia Renewable Energy Project (Phase 2)	2.19	2.19
INO	7553/3656	Eastern Indonesia Renewable Energy Project (Phase 2)	2.13	2.13
KAZ	7556/3658	Baikonyr Solar Power Project	12.00	12.00
VIE	7571/3723	Floating Solar Energy Project	20.00	20.00
PRC	7576/3750	Eco-Industrial Park Waste-to-Energy Project	100.00	100.00
THA	7579/3753	Thailand Green Bond Project	108.28	108.28
THA	7579/3754	Thailand Green Bond Project	46.40	46.40
Subtotal Nonsovereign Projects			**476.67**	**476.67**
GRAND TOTAL			**3,154.40**	**1,388.41**

ADB = Asian Development Bank, AFG = Afghanistan, BAN = Bangladesh, DMC = developing member country, IND = India, INO = Indonesia, KAZ = Kazakhstan, MON = Mongolia, MYA = Myanmar, NAU = Nauru, NEP = Nepal, PAK = Pakistan, PHI = Philippines, PRC = People's Republic of China, REG = regional, SAM = Samoa, TAJ = Tajikistan, THA = Thailand, TKM = Turkmenistan, TON = Tonga.

Source: ADB.

APPENDIX 2

ADB Projects with Energy Access Component (2008–2018)

Energy Access Investment (2008)

DMC	Loan/ Grant No.	Project Name	Total ADB Amount	Energy Access Investment
BAN	Loan 2453/2454	Public-Private Infrastructure Development Facility	165.00	34.30
PAK	Loan 2438/2439	MFF – Power Distribution Enhancement Program (Tranche 1) + grant	252.00	252.00
BHU	Loan 2463/2464	Bhutan Green Power Development Project	106.28	26.28
AFG	Grant 0134	MFF– Energy Sector Development Investment Program (Tranche 1, grant)	164.00	64.88
AFG	Grant 9128	MFF– Development of Mini Hydropower Plants in Badakshan and Bamyan Provinces (grant)	12.00	12.00
PRC	Loan 2408	Gansu Heihe Rural Hydropower Development Investment Program – Tranche 1: Erlongshan Hydropower Project	28.00	28.00
IND	Loan 7288	Rural Electrification Corporation	225.00	54.00
BHU	Loan 2463/2464	Bhutan Green Power Development Project	1.60	0.40
REG	TA 6443	Energy for All Initiative	2.30	2.30
IND	TA 7099	Integrated Renewable Energy Development	1.40	1.40
PNG	TA 7113	Power Sector Development (Town Electrification Project)	1.20	1.20
		TOTAL	**958.78**	**476.76**

AFG = Afghanistan, BAN = Bangladesh, BHU = Bhutan, DMC = developing member country , IND = India, PAK = Pakistan, PNG = Papua New Guinea, PRC = People's Republic of China, REG = regional, TA = technical assistance.
Source: ADB.

Energy Access Investment (2009)

DMC	Loan/ Grant No.	Project Name	Total ADB Amount	Energy Access Investment
SRI	Grant 0149	Clean Energy and Access Improvement	160.00	32.50
IND	Loan 0011 (MFF)	Madhya Pradesh Power Sector Investment Program (Tranche 5)	166.00	166.00
VIE	TA 7262	Renewable Energy for Remote Islands and Mountain Commune Project (Grant)	2.50	2.50
VIE	Loan 2517	Renewable Energy for Remote Islands and Mountain Commune Project	151.00	151.00
VIE	TA 7251	Quality and Safety Enhancement of Agricultural Products and Biogas Development Project-TA	1.50	1.25
VIE	Loan 2513	Quality and Safety Enhancement of Agricultural Products and Biogas Development Project	95.00	19.00
NEP	Loan 2587	Energy Access and Efficiency Improvement	65.00	32.50
LAO	TA 7241	Sustainable Natural Resource management and Productivity Enhancement Project	0.70	0.50
LAO	TA 7227	Small and Mini Hydroelectric Development Project	1.00	1.00
MON	Grant 9139	Demonstration Project for Improved Electricity Services to the Low Income Communities in Rural Areas	2.40	2.40
REG	TA 7329	Promoting Access to Renewable Energy in the Pacific	3.00	3.00
BHU	TA 7318	Rural Renewable Energy Development Project	0.90	0.90
SRI	TA 7266	Rural Household Connection	2.00	2.00
SRI	Grant 0149	Clean Energy and Access Improvement	2.20	2.20
REG	TA 7485	Effective Deployment of Distributed Small Wind Power Systems in Asian Rural Areas	3.87	3.87
		TOTAL	657.07	420.62

ADB = Asian Development Bank, BHU = Bhutan, IND = India, DMC = developing member country, LAO = Lao People's Democratic Republic, MFF = multitranche facility, MON = Mongolia, NEP – Nepal, REG = regional, SRI = Sri Lanka, TA = technical assistance, VIE = Viet Nam.
Source: ADB.

Energy Access Investment (2010)

DMC	Loan/ Grant No.	Project Name	Total ADB Amount	Energy Access Investment
LAO	Grant 0195	Greater Mekong Subregion Northern Power Transmission (Grant)	20.00	20.00
INO	Loan 2619	Java-Bali Electricity Distribution Performance Improvement	50.00	50.00
AFG	Equity 7307	Sungas LPG Project (Distribution Network)	8.00	8.00
BAN	Loan 2622/2623	Natural Gas Access Improvement Project (formerly Clean Fuel Development Project)	266.00	39.00
PRC	Loan 2632	Integrated Renewable Biomass Energy Development Project (formerly Rural Energy and Ecosystem Rehabilitation) (Phase II)	66.08	66.08
PRC	Loan 2260	Inner Mongolia Autonomous Region Environment Improvement Project	150.00	150.00
RMI	Grant 9148	Improved Energy Supply to Poor Households	1.80	1.80
IND	Loan 2681	Bihar Power System Improvement Project & TA	132.50	132.50
BHU	Grant 022	Rural Renewable Energy Development (Grant)	21.59	21.59
PRC	Loan 2693	Municipal Natural Gas Infrastructure Development Project (Phase 2)	200.00	200.00
PNG	Loan 3544	Town Electrification Investment Program	57.30	57.30
PAK	Loan 2726	MFF - Renewable Energy Development Sector Investment Program PFR2	200.00	200.00
		TOTAL	**1,173.27**	**946.27**

ADB = Asian Development Bank, AFG = Afghanistan, BAN = Bangladesh, BHU = Bhutan, DMC = developing member country, IND = India, INO = Indonesia, LAO = Lao People's Democratic Republic, PAK = Pakistan, PNG = Papua New Guinea, PRC = People's Republic of China, RMI = Republic of the Marshall Islands.
Source: ADB.

Energy Access Investment (2011)

DMC	Loan/Grant No.	Project Name	Total ADB Amount	Energy Access Investment
IND	Project No. 44941	Solar Power Generation Guarantee	150.00	17.02
REG	TA 7914	Harnessing Climate Change Mitigation Initiatives to Benefit Women	2.70	2.70
IND	Project No. 43464	Himachal Pradesh Clean Energy Transmission Investment Program	0.60	0.12
IND	Loan 2794	Himachal Pradesh Clean Energy Transmission - Tranche 1	113.00	88.76
NEP	Loan 2808	Electricity Transmission Expansion and Supply Improvement Project	56.00	6.43
SRI	Loan 2733/2734	Sustainable Power Sector Support	120.00	23.34
AFG	Grant 0377	MFF - Energy Sector Development Investment Program-Project 3 (formerly MFF - Energy Sector Enhancement Investment Program-Project III)	43.00	38.00
IND		Enhancing Energy-Based Livelihoods for Women and Entrepreneurs	1.00	1.00
UZB	Loan 2779	Advance Electricity Metering Project	150.00	150.00
PAK	Loan 2972	MFF Power Transmission and Distribution Enhancement T3	243.24	243.24
IND	Loan 2764	MFF - Madhya Pradesh Energy Efficiency Project (Tranche 1)	200.00	200.00
IND	Loan 2800	Assam Power Sector Enhancement Investment Program - Tranche 3	50.00	39.82
IND	Loan 2830	Madhya Pradesh Energy Efficiency Improvement Investment Program - Tranche 2	200.00	200.00
REG	TA 7833	Capacity Building for the Efficient Utilization of Biomass for Bioenergy and Food	4.00	4.00
BAN	Grant 0253/0254	Public-Private Infrastructure Development Facility (Supplement)	3.30	2.00
PHI	TA 7781	Rural Community-Based Renewable Energy Development in Mindanao	2.00	2.00
BAN	Loan 2769	Power System Efficiency Improvement Project	300.00	16.30
SOL	TA 8048	Renewable Energy for Telecom Networks	0.40	0.14
		TOTAL	**1,639.24**	**1,034.75**

ADB = Asian Development Bank, AFG = Afghanistan, BAN = Bangladesh, DMC = developing member country, IND = India, NEP = Nepal, PAK = Pakistan, PHI = Philippines, REG = regional, SOL = Solomon Islands, SRI = Sri Lanka, TA = technical assistance, UZB = Uzbekistan, VIE = Viet Nam.

Source: ADB.

Energy Access Investment (2012)

DMC	Loan/ Grant No.	Project Name	Total ADB Amount	Energy Access Investment
UZB	Loan 2918/2917	Namangan 500-Kilovolt Power Transmission Project	288.00	150.00
PRC	Loan 2898	Heilongjiang Energy Efficiency and Urban Environment Improvement Project	150.00	150.00
PRC	Loan 2885	Shanxi Energy Efficiency and Urban Environment Improvement Project	100.00	100.00
CAM	Loan 2979	Medium Voltage Sub-Transmission Expansion Sector Project	45.00	45.00
SRI	Grant 0303	Clean Energy and Network Efficiency Enhancement	1.50	1.00
SRI	Loan 2892/2893	Clean Energy and Network Efficiency Enhancement	131.50	117.00
PNG	Grant 0288/9163	Improved Energy Access for Rural Communities	5.00	5.00
AFG		MFF - Energy Sector Development Investment Program-Project 4 (formerly MFF - Energy Development Project Tranche 4)	200.00	40.00
VIE	Loan 2968	Low-Carbon Agricultural Support Project	84.00	84.00
PAK	Loan 2972	MFF Power Distribution Enhancement Investment Program-Tranche 3	245.00	245.00
TON	TA 7940	Outer Island Renewable Energy Project (Additional Financing)	0.23	0.23
SOL	TA 8130	Outer Island Renewable Energy Project	0.75	0.75
SOL	TA 8130	Outer Island Renewable Energy Project (Additional Financing)	0.25	0.25
TON	TA 8296	Outer Island Energy Efficiency Project	0.40	0.40
VAN	TA 8285	Energy Access Project	0.75	0.75
SAM	TA 8308	Preparing the Renewable Energy Project	0.75	0.75
UZB	TA 8142	Takhiatash Power Plant Efficiency Improvement Project	1.20	1.20
KAZ	TA 8253	Karaganda District Heating Network Rehabilitation Project (formerly Energy Efficiency Project)	1.00	1.00
		TOTAL	**1,255.33**	**942.33**

ADB = Asian Development Bank, AFG = Afghanistan, CAM = Cambodia, DMC = developing member country, KAZ = Kazakhstan, PAK = Pakistan, PHI = Philippines, PNG = Papua New Guinea, PRC = People's Republic of China, REG = regional, SAM = Samoa, SOL = Solomon Islands, SRI = Sri Lanka, TA = technical assistance, TON = Tonga, UZB = Uzbekistan, VAN = Vanuatu, VIE = Viet Nam.
Source: ADB.

Energy Access Investment (2013)

DMC	Loan/ Grant No.	Project Name	Total ADB Amount	Energy Access Investment
IND	Loan 7381	Off grid pay-as-you-go solar power	2.00	2.00
CAM	Grant 336	Rural Energy Project	6.11	6.11
NEP	Loan 2990/2991	Tanahu Hydropower Project	150.00	8.00
PNG	Loan 2998/2999	Port Moresby Powergrid	66.70	8.10
IND	Loan 3001	Himachal Pradesh Clean Energy Transmission Investment Program-Tranche2	110.00	110.00
TAJ	Grant 0346/ TA 8394	Access to Green Finance Project	10.75	7.53
TON	Grant 0347/0348	Outer Island Renewable Energy Project	6.50	6.50
REG	TA 7329	Promoting Access to Renewable Energy in the Pacific (Supplementary)	0.10	0.10
INO	Loan 3015	West Kalimantan Power Grid Strengthening	101.00	101.00
KAZ	Loan 3018/3019	Akmola Electricity Distribution Network Modernization and Expansion Project	40.00	40.00
MYA	Loan 3084	Power Improvement Distribution Project	60.00	60.00
IND	Loan 7398	BSES Radjhani Power Limited Delhi Electricity Distribution System Improvement	80.00	80.00
IND	Loan 3066	Madhya Pradesh Power Transmission and Distribution System Improvement Project	350.00	98.74
BAN	Loan 3045/3046	Second Public-Private Infrastructure Development Facility, Tranche 2	110.00	10.00
BAN	Loan 3087	Power System Expansion and Efficiency Improvement Investment Program - Tranche 2	310.00	270.64
REG	TA 7512	Empowering the poor through increasing access to Energy (Supplemental)	4.98	4.98
INO	Ta 8287	Scaling up Renewable Energy Access in Eastern Indonesia	3.00	3.00
IND	Loan 3052/8275, TA 8486	Rajasthan Renewable Energy Transmission Investment Program - Tranche 1	152.00	0.50
PAK	Loan 3096	Power Distribution Enhancement Program, Tranche 4	167.20	167.20
NEP	Loan 3057	Bagmati River Basin Improvement Project	30.00	
		TOTAL	**1,760.34**	**984.40**

ADB = Asian Development Bank, BAN = Bangladesh, CAM = Cambodia, DMC = developing member country, IND = India, INO = Indonesia, KAZ = Kazakhstan, MYA = Myanmar, NEP = Nepal, PAK = Pakistan, REG = regional, SOL = Solomon Islands, SRI = Sri Lanka, TA = technical assistance, VAN = Vanuatu.

Source: ADB.

Energy Access Investment (2014)

DMC	Loan/ Grant No.	Project Name	Total ADB Amount	Energy Access Investment
MYA	TA 8657	Off-Grid Renewable Energy Demonstration Project	2.00	2.00
SOL	Grant 0386/Loan 3127	Provincial Renewable Energy Project	12.00	12.00
NEP	TA 8678/Loan 3139	South Asia Subregional Economic Cooperation Power System Expansion Project	251.20	63.90
SRI	Loan 3146/3147	Green Power Development and Energy Efficiency Improvement Investment Program-Tranche 1	300.00	22.77
IND	Loan 3140	Assam Power Sector Investment Program-Tranche 1	300.00	50.00
MLD	Grant 0409/0410	Preparing Outer Island for Sustainable energy development Proj	50.00	50.00
COO	Loan 3193	Renewable Energy Sector Project	11.19	11.19
IND	Loan 3200	Assam Power Sector Investment Program-Tranche 4	50.20	37.30
PRC	Loan 3218	Low-Carbon District Heating Project in Hohhot in Inner Mongolia Autonomous Region	150.00	150.00
		TOTAL	**1,126.59**	**399.16**

ADB = Asian Development Bank, COO = Cook Islands, DMC = developing member country, IND = India, MLD = Maldives, MYA = Myanmar, NEP = Nepal, PRC = People's Republic of China, SRI = Sri Lanka, TA = technical assistance, UZB = Uzbekistan.
Source: ADB.

Energy Access Investment (2015)

DMC	Loan/ Grant No.	Project Name	Total ADB Amount	Energy Access Investment
REG	CDTA 0017	Promoting Sustainable Energy for All in Asia and the Pacific	7.74	7.74
BAN	TA 8927	Bangladesh: Enabling Poor Women's Benefits from Enhanced Access to Energy in Hatiya Island	0.50	0.50
IND	Loan 8298	Off-Grid Prepaid Solar Leasing Project	6.00	6.00
SRI	TA 8952	Supporting Electricity Supply Reliability Improvement	0.23	0.23
PRC	Loan 3358	Qingdao Smart Low-Carbon District Energy	130.00	130.00
INO	Loan 3339/8297	Electricity Grid Strengthening-Sumatra Program	600.00	372.00
UZB	Loan 3286	Advanced Electricity Metering Phase 4 Project	300.00	300.00
VIE	TA 9008	Rural Electrification	1.00	1.00
TON	Grant 0444/0445/0446	Outer Island Renewable Energy-Additional Financing	5.76	5.76
PAK	Loan 3328/3329	Second Power Distribution Enhancement Investment Program-Tranche 1	400.00	400.00
MLD	Grant 0409/0410/0429	Preparing Outer Islands for Sustainable Energy Additional Financing	5.00	5.00
PNG	Grant 0469	Town Electrification Investment Program, Tranche 1, Additional Financing	4.80	4.50
		TOTAL	**1,461.03**	**1,232.73**

ADB = Asian Development Bank, BAN = Bangladesh, CDTA = capacity development technical assistance, DMC = developing member country, IND = India, INO = Indonesia, MLD = Maldives, PAK = Pakistan, PNG = Papua New Guinea, PRC = People's Republic of China, REG = regional, SRI = Sri Lanka, TA = technical assistance, TON = Tonga, UZB = Uzbekistan, VIE = Viet Nam.
Source: ADB.

Energy Access Investment (2016)

DMC	Loan/Grant No.	Project Name	Total ADB Amount	Energy Access Investment
AZE	MFF 0091	Power Distribution Enhancement Investment Program	250.00	250.00
SRI	Loan 3409	Supporting Electricity Supply Reliability Improvement	115.00	115.00
PAK	Loan 3476	Access to Clean Energy Investment Program	325.70	325.75
AFG	Grant 0521	Energy Supply Improvement Investment Program-Tranche 2 (Formerly Multitranche Financing Facility II: Energy Development 2014-2023)	188.23	11.20
SRI	Loan 3483	Green Power Development and Energy Efficiency Improvement Investment Program-Tranche 2	150.00	23.25
TON	Grant 0258/ Loan 3509	Outer Island Renewable Energy Project-Additional Financing	5.00	5.00
SOL	Grant 0514	Solar Power Development Project	8.44	8.44
TAJ	TA 8945	CAREC Corridors 2, 5, and 6 (Dushanbe–Kurgonteppa) Road Project	3.50	0.44
PRC	Loan 3406	Inner Mongolia Saikexing Breeding and Biotechnology Group Sustainable Dairy Farming and Milk Safety Project	62.50	2.73
		Total	**1,108.37**	**741.81**

ADB = Asian Development Bank, AFG = Afghanistan, AZE = Azerbaijan, DMC = developing member country, PRC = People's Republic of China, SOL = Solomon Islands, SRI = Sri Lanka, TA = technical assistance, TAJ = Tajikistan, TON = Tonga.
Source: ADB.

Energy Access Investment (2017)

DMC	Loan/ Grant No.	Project Name	Total ADB Amount	Energy Access Investment
NEP	Loan 3452	Power Transmission and Distribution Efficiency Enhancement Project	150.00	85.81
INO	Loan 3560	Sustainable Energy Access in Eastern Indonesia Electricity Grid Development Program	600.00	600.00
VAN	Grant 0543/0544, Loan 3572	Energy Access Project	12.00	12.00
BAN	Loan 3522/3523	Bangladesh Power System Enhancement and Efficiency Improvement Project	616.00	512.32
ARM	Loan 3540	Distribution Network Rehabilitation, Efficiency Improvement, and Augmentation	80.00	80.00
		TOTAL	**1,458.00**	**1,290.13**

ADB = Asian Development Bank, ARM = Armenia, BAN = Bangladesh, INO = Indonesia, NEP = Nepal, VAN = Vanuatu.
Source: ADB.

Energy Access Investment (2018)

DMC	Loan/ Grant No.	Project Name	Total ADB Amount	Energy Access Investment
TON	Grant 0575	Cyclone Gita Recovery Project	6.80	6.80
MON	Loan 3648	Ulaanbaatar Air Quality Improvement	130.00	6.08
MYA	Loan 3748	Power Network Development Project	298.90	103.97
BAN	Grant 053/054	Power System Efficiency Improvement (Off-Grid Solar Photovoltaic Pumping Systems Component) - Additional Financing	25.44	25.44
TON	Grant 056/057/058	Outer Island Renewable Energy	8.88	8.88
PRC	Loan 3765	Air Quality Improvement in the Greater Beijing–Tianjin–Hebei Region—Shandong Clean Heating and Cooling Project	399.91	399.91
		TOTAL	869.93	550.27

ADB = Asian Development Bank, BAN = Bangladesh, MON = Mongolia, MYA = Myanmar, PRC = People's Republic of China, TON = Tonga.
Source: ADB.

APPENDIX 3

Solar Projects Supported Under Asia Solar Energy Initiative (2010–2018)

Operations	DMC	Project Name	Total Loan/ Grant Amount ($ million)	Approval Date	MW Installed	MW Supported	Total MW Catalyzed
Private	THA	Natural Energy Devt Company (Solar Power Project)	70.00	16-Apr-10	55.0	–	55.0
	PHI	0.567 MW Solar Power Rooftop Plant at ADB Headquarters	0.06	12-Jun-10	0.6	–	0.6
Private	THA	Bangchak Petroleum Public Company (BCP)-Bangchak Solar Power Project	134.31	05-Oct-10	44.5	–	44.5
Private	IND	Solar Power Generation	150.00	19-Apr-11	130.0	–	130.0
Public	BAN	Power System Efficiency Improvement Project	300.00	11-Aug-11	6.0	–	6.0
Public	IND	Gujarat Solar Power Transmission Project	100.00	12-Sep-11		500.0	500.0
Private	IND	Dahanu Solar Power Private Limited	48.00	02-Nov-11	40.0	–	40.0
Private	IND	Rajasthan Concentrating Solar Power Project (Rajasthan Sun Technique Energy Private Ltd)	103.00	29-Mar-12	100.0	–	100.0
Private	THA	Bangchak Solar Energy Company Ltd (Provincial Solar Power Project)	37.80	25-Jun-12	32.0	–	32.0
Private	IND	145-MW Grid-Connected Solar Project (5 projects combined)	100.00	18-Sep-12	145.0	–	145.0
Public	SRI	Clean Energy and Network Improvement Project	30.00	18-Sep-12	1.0	–	1.0
Public	PHI	Market Transformation through Introduction of Energy Efficient Electric Vehicle Project	5.00	11-Dec-12	1.0	–	1.0
Private	IND	Simpa Networks Off-Grid-Pay-As-You-Go Solar Power	2.00	15-Jan-13	2.5	–	2.5
Private	THA	Solarco Company Ltd.	85.00	12-Apr-13	57.0	–	57.0
Public	FSM	Yap Renewable Energy Development Project	9.04	20-Jun-13	0.3	–	0.3

continued on next page

Table continued

Operations	DMC	Project Name	Total Loan/ Grant Amount ($ million)	Approval Date	MW Installed	MW Supported	Total MW Catalyzed
Public	TON	Outer Island RE Project	2.00	27-Jun-13	1.3	–	1.3
Public	IND	Rajasthan RE Transmission Investment Program	300.00	26-Sep-13		1,250.0	1,250.0
Public	BAN	Second Public-Private Infrastructure Development Facility	10.00	17-Oct-13	3.3	–	3.33
Public	UZB	Samarkand Solar Power Project	110.00	20-Nov-13	100.0	–	100.0
Public	PRC	Qinghai Delingha CSP Project	150.00	02-Dec-13	50.0	–	50.0
Private	IND	Welspun Renewable Energy Limited-Solar and Wind Power Development	36.41	12-Dec-13	200.0	–	200.0
Public	NEP	South Asia Subregional Economic Cooperation Power System Expansion	–	04-Jul-14	4.8	–	4.8
Public	MLD	Preparing Outer Islands for Sustainable Energy Development	38.00	29-Sep-14	21.0	–	21.0
Private	IND	ACME-EDF Solar Power Project	100.00	16-Oct-14	200.0	–	200.0
Public	COO	Renewable Energy Sector	11.09	21-Nov-14	3.2	–	3.2
Private	IND	Simpa Energy Private Limited (Off-Grid Prepaid Solar Leasing Project)	6.00	01-Dec-15	44.4	–	44.4
Public	IND	Accelerating Infrastructure Investment Facility in India-Tranche 2	–	30-Oct-15	30.0	–	30.0
Private	IND	Mytrah Aadhya Power Pvt. Limited	14.00	22-Mar-16	50.0	–	50.0
Private	IND	Mytrah Aakash Power Pvt. Limited	14.00	22-Mar-16	50.0	–	50.0
Private	THA	Stumpf Energy Solutions (Thailand) and Stumpf Energy Tranche B (Distributed Commercial Solar Power)	47.00	10-Aug-16	100.0	–	100.0
Private	CAM	Sunseap Asset (Cambodia) Co. Ltd. (Cambodia Solar Power)	3.60	07-Dec-16	10.0	–	10.0
Private	CAM	Sunseap Asset (Cambodia) Co. Ltd. (Cambodia Solar Power)	3.25	07-Dec-16	–	–	–
Private	IND	ReNew Private Ventures Private Limited (ReNew Clean Energy Project)	102.30	02-Dec-16	398.0	–	398.0

continued on next page

Table continued

Operations	DMC	Project Name	Total Loan/ Grant Amount ($ million)	Approval Date	MW Installed	MW Supported	Total MW Catalyzed
Private	THA	Thai-Sunseap Asset Company Limited (Grid Parity Rooftop Solar Project)	43.56	02-Dec-16	100.0	–	100.0
Public	SRI	Supporting Electricity Supply Reliability Improvement	115.00	26-Jul-16	1.2	–	1.2
Public	SOL	Solar Power Development Project	2.24	21-Nov-16	2.0	–	2.0
Public	PAK	Access to Clean Energy Investment Project	300.00	25-Nov-16	182.0	–	182.0
Public	NEP	South Asia Subregional Economic Cooperation Power System Expansion-Additional financing	20.00	29-Dec-16	25.0	–	25.0
Public	AFG	Energy Supply Improvement Investment Program (Solar), Tranche 3	44.76	29-Sep-17	20.0	–	20.0
Public	PRC	Air Quality Improvement in the Greater Beijing-Tianjin-Hebei Region—Regional Emission Reduction and Pollution Control Facility	500.00	14-Dec-17	425.0	–	425.0
Private	SAM	Solar Power Development	2.00	04-Aug-17	4.0	–	4.0
Public	IND	Solar Transmission Sector Project	175.00	29-Mar-17		4,200.0	4,200.0
Public	SRI	Rooftop Solar Power Generation Project	50.00	26-Sep-17	50.0	–	50.0
Private	PAK	Zorlu Solar Power Project	20.00	23-Nov-17	100.0	–	100.0
Private	INO	PT Energi Bayu Jeneponto (Eastern Indonesia Renewable Energy – Phase 1)	56.40	29-Nov-17	72.0	–	72.0
Private	REG	ASEAN Distributed Power Project 1	75.00	17-May-17	100.0	–	100.0
Private	REG	ASEAN Distributed Power Project 2	235.00	29-Sep-17	100.0	–	100.0
Public	MON	Upscaling Renewable energy Sector	40.00	20-Sep-18	41.0	–	41.0
Private	INO	PY Infrastruktur Terbarukan Lestari(Eastern Indonesia Renewable Energy Project (Phase 2)	12.50	11-Apr-18	42.0	–	42.0
Private	KAZ	Baikonyr Solar Limited Liability Partnership (Baikonyr Solar Power)	12.00	10-May-18	50.0	–	50.0

continued on next page

Table continued

Operations	DMC	Project Name	Total Loan/ Grant Amount ($ million)	Approval Date	MW Installed	MW Supported	Total MW Catalyzed
Private	THA	B. Grimm Public Company Limited (Thailand Green bond)	154.70	05-Dec-18	98.5	–	98.5
Private	VIE	Da Nhim-Ham Thuan-Dami Hydro Power Joint Stock Company (Floating Solar Energy)	20.00	04-Oct-18	47.5	–	47.5
TOTAL					3,341.1	5,950.0	9,291.1

– = not applicable, AFG = Afghanistan, BAN = Bangladesh, CAM = Cambodia, COO = Cook Islands, FSM = Federated States of Micronesia, IND = India, INO = Indonesia, KAZ = Kazakhstan, MLD = Maldives, MW = megawatt, MON = Mongolia, NEP = Nepal, PHI = Philippines, PRC = People's Republic of China, RE = renewable energy, REG = Regional, SAM = Samoa, SRI = Sri Lanka, THA = Thailand, TON = Tonga, VIE = Viet Nam.
Source: ADB.

References

Asian Development Bank (ADB). 1995. *Asian Development Bank Annual Report 1995.* Manila. https://www.adb.org/sites/default/files/institutional-document/32137/adb-ar-1995.pdf.

———. 1995. *Bank Policy for the Energy Sector.* Manila.

———. 1996. *Asian Development Bank Annual Report 2016.* Manila. https://www.adb.org/sites/default/files/institutional-document/32137/adb-ar-1995.pdf.

———. 2000. *Energy 2000 Review of the Energy Policy of the Asian Development Bank.* Manila.

———. 2001. *Moving the Poverty Reduction Agenda Forward in Asia and the Pacific: The Long-Term Strategic Framework of the Asian Development Bank (2001-2015).* Manila. http://hdl.handle.net/11540/5467.

———. 2008a. *2008 Strategy 2020: The Long-Term Strategic Framework of the Asian Development Bank 2008-2020.* Manila. https://www.adb.org/sites/default/files/institutional-document/32121/strategy2020-print.pdf.

———. 2008b. *Technical Assistance for the Energy for All Initiative.* Manila. https://www.adb.org/projects/40629-012/main#project-pds.

———. 2009a. *Energy Policy 2009.* Manila. https://www.adb.org/sites/default/files/institutional-document/32032/energy-policy-2009.pdf.

———. 2009b. *Technical Assistance for Effective Deployment of Distributed Small Wind Power Systems in Asian Rural Areas.* Manila. https://www.adb.org/projects/43458-012/main#project-pds.

———. 2010a. *Technical Assistance for Empowering the Poor through Increasing Access to Energy.* Manila. https://www.adb.org/projects/43385-022/main#projects-pds.

———. 2010b. *Technical Assistance for Knowledge Platform Development for the Asia Solar Energy Initiative.* Manila. https://www.adb.org/projects/44233-012/main#project-pds.

———. 2011a. *Indicators for the Asian Development Bank Energy Sector Operations (2005-2010).* Manila. https://www.adb.org/sites/default/files/publication/29435/indicators-energy-operations.pdf.

———. 2011b. *Technical Assistance for Quantum Leap in Wind Power Development in Asia and the Pacific.* Manila. https://www.adb.org/projects/44489-012/main#project-pds.

———. 2011c. *Technical Assistance for Establishing a Pilot Center to Facilitate Climate Technology Investments in Asia and the Pacific – Promotion of Investment in Climate Technology Products through Venture Capital Funds.* Manila. https://www.adb.org/projects/45134-004/main#project-pds.

———. 2015. *Clean Energy Program: Accelerating Low-Carbon Development in Asia and the Pacific Region.* Manila. https://www.adb.org/sites/default/files/publication/28995/clean-energy-program-brochure.pdf.

———. 2018. *Strategy 2030: Achieving a Prosperous, Inclusive, Resilient, and Sustainable Asia and the Pacific.* Manila. https://www.adb.org/sites/default/files/institutional-document/435391/strategy-2030-main-document.pdf.

———. Carbon Storage and Fund. https://www.adb.org/site/funds/funds/carbon-capture-storage-fund.

Bloomberg New Energy Finance. 2018. *Clean Energy Investment Trends 2017.* https://data.bloomberglp.com/bnef/sites/14/2018/01/BNEF-Clean-Energy-Investment-Investment-Trends-2017.pdf.

———. 2019. Clean Energy Investments Exceeded $300 Billion Once Again in 2019. https://about.bnef.com/blog/clean-energy-investment-exceeded-300-billion-2018/

International Energy Agency. 2018. *World Energy Outlook 2018: Scenarios.* https://www.iea.org/weo2018/scenarios/.

———. 2019. *World Energy Investments 2019.* Paris.

———. Electricity Access Database. https://www.iea.org/sdg/electricity/.

———. Clean Cooking Database. https://www.iea.org/sdg/cooking/.

International Renewable Energy Agency. 2017. *Renewable Power: Sharply Falling Generation Costs.* https://www.irena.org/-/media/Files/IRENA/Agency/Publication/2017/Nov/%20IRENA_Sharply_falling_costs_2017.pdf.

Renewable Energy Policy Network for the 21st Century. 2018. *Renewables 2018: Global Status Report.* Paris.

———. 2019. *Renewables 2019: Global Status Report.* Paris.

United Nations. *Sustainable Development Goals.* https://www.un.org/sustainabledevelopment/sustainable-development-goals/.

———. United Nations Framework Convention on Climate Change. *The Paris Agreement.* https://unfccc.int/process-and-meetings/the-paris-agreement/the-paris-agreement.

Lightning Source UK Ltd.
Milton Keynes UK
UKHW050729070620
364510UK00008B/200